Islamic Banking Challenges in Indian Banks

By,
Hareem Tariq

CONTENTS

Declaration		*i*
Certificate		*ii*
Acknowledgement		*iii-iv*
Table of Contents		*v*
List of Tables		*vi-vii*
List of Figures		*viii*
List of Abbreviations		*ix-x*
List of Glossary		*xi-xii*
CHAPTER I	INTRODUCTION	1-28
CHAPTER II	LITERATURE REVIEW AND RESEARCH METHODOLOGY	29-64
CHAPTER III	BANKING SYSTEM IN INDIA: A SYNOPTIC VIEW	65-94
CHAPTER IV	ISLAMIC BANKING: CONCEPT AND GLOBAL PRACTICES	95-128
CHAPTER V	CHALLENGES FOR ISLAMIC BANKING IN INDIA: EXPECTED FRAMEWORK	129-159
CHAPTER VI	PROSPECTS OF ISLAMIC BANKING IN INDIA	160-188
CHAPTER VII	CONCLUSION AND SUGGESTIONS	189-208
	APPENDICES	
	BIBLIOGRAPHY	

LIST OF TABLES

S.No.	Table No.	Title of The Table	Page No.
1	4.1	Financial Performance of Barkat Investment Group (1988-1998)	107
2	4.2	Financial Performance of Baitun Nasr (1977-1999)	109
3	4.3	Financial Performance of Al-Najib Milli Mutual Benefits Limited (1993-1999)	110
4	4.4	Financial Highlights of Al-Barr Finance House Limited (1990-1999)	111
5	4.5	List of Shariah Compliant Funds	118
6	6.1	Reliability Analysis of the Variable Awareness (item wise)	161
7	6.2	Reliability Analysis of Motivational Factors (item wise)	162
8	6.3	Reliability Analysis of Attitude of People (item wise)	163
9	6.4	Reliability Analysis of Variable Implementation on item wise	163
10	6.5	Reliability Analysis of Variable Application (item wise)	164
11	6.6	Overall Reliability Measures of the Study	164
12	6.7	Gender Classification of Respondents	167
13	6.8	Classification of Respondents on the Basis of Age	168
14	6.9	Classification of Respondents on the Basis of Educational Qualification	169
15	6.10	Classification of Respondents on the Basis of Occupation	170
16	6.11	Classification of Respondents on the Basis of Religion	171
17	6.12	Assessing Awareness of Islamic Banking	172
18	6.13	Assessing Impact of Education Level in Application of Islamic Banking	174
19	6.14	Difference of Attitude in Different Groups of Education	174
20	6.15	Difference in Application of Islamic Banking Methods Among Muslims and People from Other Communities	175
21	6.16	Muslims are Giving in Charity the Interest Received from the Banks or Not	176
22	6.17	Muslims are taking Measures to Avoid Interest	176

23	6.18	Difference of getting affected by motivating factors of Islamic banking in Muslims and Others	177
24	6.19	Practice of Qard hasana	180
25	6.20	Level of Awareness of terminologies of Islamic Methods of Finance and Banking	181
26	6.21	Utilization of Interest	182
27	6.22	Interest from Commercial Banks are Given in Charity	183
28	6.23	People Utilizing the Interest Money for Personal Use	184
29	6.24	Preference to Interest Free Schemes for Investment Purpose	185

CHAPTER-1

INTRODUCTION

The present chapter is devoted to the introduction of the theme of research on possibilities of zero interest banking system as given in Sharia System in Islam, in India keeping in view the legal framework and various limitations.

1.1 Introduction

Bank as is understood in general terms is a depositor or lender for the safekeeping of money. With the changing times banks are performing a host of other financial services like insurance, mutual funds, securities, etc. It is important to look at some definitions of banks to understand the concept of bank.

"An institution that provides a great variety of financial services. At their most basic, banks hold money on behalf of customers, which is payable on demand, either by appearing at the bank for a withdrawal or by writing a check to a third party. Banks use the money they hold to finance loans, which they make to businesses and individuals to pay for operations, mortgages, education expenses, and any number of things. Many banks also perform other services for a fee; for instance they offer certified checks to customers guaranteeing payment to third parties. In some countries they may provide investment and insurance services. With the exception of Zero Interest based banks, they pay interest on deposits and receive interest on their loans. Banks are regulated by the laws and central banks of their home countries; normally they must receive a charter to engage in business. Banks are usually organised as corporations." (Farlex financial dictionary- Bank)

Definition of Bank: "Commercial banks are mainly concerned with managing withdrawals and deposits as well as supplying short-term loans to individuals and small businesses. Consumers primarily use these banks for basic checking and savings accounts, certificates of deposit and sometimes for home mortgages." (Investopedia - Bank)

With an understanding of the concept of banking it is also to be noticed that banking industry has seen a sea change from what it was in India and in today's world where everything is available at the touch of a button and information of everything can be accessed easily by anyone, and every system has seen a sea change for what it was a few decades ago, so the banking system now has reached to every part of the country, where the industry is providing various financial services from safe keeping of money, gold, managing investments, mutual funds, stocks, insurance, financing house, automobile and other projects. The banking system has evolved a lot worldwide and in India as well, with e banking and mobile banking people can do a lot of transactions even without physically visiting the bank. These days a lot of products which were not available are easily available due to globalization, as the Italian Pizza, pasta, has made way to our homes, international brands of apparel, food outlets have made a say in India and have been successful, and the banking system can also be amended as per the needs of the customers in our country. The banking system works on a traditional system wherein the bank's earnings are mainly through interest which it charges in its dealings. But still there is a substantial amount of population which is undesirable to deal in interest and thus avoid interest whether they have to pay or earn. India being home to 180 million Muslims, thus the government of India needs to recognize and implement the requirements of the people and work consequently for them. Actually it is not only in Islam that interest is prohibited but also in early scriptures of Hinduism interest was unacceptable.

Participation in usury was forbidden in Brahmin and Kshatriya varnas by Vashishtha. Usury (interest) became more acceptable by 2nd century CE. The Manusmriti considered usury as means of acquiring wealth or for living a livelihood and this also became acceptable. It also considered money lending above a certain rate and having different ceiling rates for different castes as a grave sin.

It can be made clear with an example, if a person wants to start up a business and he has some good project and he is unsure of his income, but he needs money and approaches the bank and bank is ready to give him loan but asks to repay from the very next month in instalment with interest, what should he do as he does not have any other option, he will take the loan but if in case he is not able to make any profits in first few months, which will make him unable to pay his instalments which will further increase his debt and now, instead of concentrating on his business he will now be focusing how to repay the loan as it is increasing due to the amount of interest present in it, even if he is able to pay single instalment still, the principal amount would remain unpaid and more and more interest amount is increasing. This will ultimately lead to depression, anxiety and finally to suicide and farmer suicides is not a new thing in India. Business involves risk and uncertainty thus the one providing loan needs to keep in mind this, that it is being contributed for the betterment of the society as a whole and when there will be profits pouring, they will be making good amount of money and can always charge for the services which are being provided.

Zero Interest based Banking or Interest free banking is a system of banking which functions as per the rules of Sharia (Islamic Law) as per which riba (interest) is prohibited in financial transactions. According to Islam one cannot earn money with money, as this leads to exploitation of the masses and inequality in the society. In actual practice in India if a person is in need of money he approaches a bank, he will be funded but would have to pay the principal amount and the interest amount which is divided in monthly or yearly instalments, so the total sum of money which he is paying to the bank is generally quite high. This practice leads to rich becoming richer and poor becoming poorer and thus, results in inequality in the society. For this particular reason, interest is prohibited in Islam and as per Sharia riba (interest) is a tool of oppression and is actually a means to unjustly take the money of others by exploiting their needs and circumstances. Thus, a riba based system is forbidden and charity as an alternative is promoted. "And their taking of *Riba* (usury or interest) though they were forbidden from taking it and their devouring of men's substance wrongfully (bribery, etc.). And we have prepared for the disbelievers among them a painful torment". Quran 4:161 [Al-Nisa]

1.2 Features of Zero Interest Based Banking

Zero Interest based banking principles have a basis of the philosophies and principles outlined in the Quran and the Sunnah of Prophet Muhammad ☐. So the terms which were used back then have been retained and some more concepts have been added for the present day sustenance. Thus Zero Interest based banking was very much there 1400 years ago. Today what is known as Islamic Banking came into existence around 1963. The Zero Interest based banking works on Profit and- Loss Sharing (PLS) model which had been a pioneer in 1963 with the name of an Egyptian Savings Bank called as Mit Ghamr. Though, the very first commercial Zero Interest based bank of the world was considered to be Dubai Islamic Bank (DIB) which was founded in 1975. Now, it is important to know about some financial activities performed by the Islamic banks and how the element of interest can be eliminated, by having an insight of the cost structure of a bank. The following is the discussion on the host of financial activities performed by an Islamic bank which have been given by Gafoor (2005):

1. Deposit accounts

As commercial banks have deposit accounts similarly Zero Interest based banks also have three kinds of deposit accounts: current, savings and investments.

- Current accounts

Current or demand deposit accounts are almost the same as in all commercial banks. Deposit is guaranteed in such accounts.

- Savings accounts

Savings accounts have a difference as from the current account and are practiced in different forms. Like, in some of the banks, the depositors permit the banks to use their funds but they gain an assurance of getting the entire amount back from the bank and banks implement a number of modes to suggest their clientele to deposit with them, but do not promise any profit. In others, savings accounts are treated as investment accounts but with less strict terms with reference to the conditions of withdrawals and minimum balance. Capital is not guaranteed by the banks but care is taken that investment from such accounts should be made in relatively risk-free short-term projects. Low profits are expected only on a portion of the average minimum balance as a high level of reserves needs to be set aside at all times to meet withdrawal demands of the clients.

- Investment account

In investment accounts investment deposits are accepted for either a fixed period or unlimited period and the investors agree in advance to share the profit (or loss) in a given proportion with the bank. Capital is not guaranteed in such an arrangement.

Banks usually adopt many types of modes to acquire assets or finance projects. But they can be broadly classified into three areas: investment, trade and lending.

2. Investment financing

This is done in three ways:

a) *Musharaka* it is an agreement where a bank joins another firm for setting up a joint venture, both parties participate in various steps and aspects of the project according to their capabilities. The profit and loss are shared in a pre agreed term. This is very much like a joint venture. This venture is an independent legal entity and gradually the bank can withdraw after the initial period.

b) *Mudarabha* is an arrangement where the bank is the financier and the client is providing the expertise, management and labor. Here also the sharing of profits are in a pre agreed proportion, but in case of losses the bank has to bear it.

c) Estimated rate of return as the base of financing: In this scheme, the bank first estimates the expected rate of return on a specific project and then financing is done on the basis that at least that rate (which is negotiable) should be paid to the bank. If the project has more profit than expected rate then the excess amount goes to the client and if the profit is less than the estimated rate the bank will accept the lower rate. In case there is a loss the bank will have to share it.

3. Trade Financing

Trade Financing is done in various ways; the main types are discussed below:

a) Mark-up financing -the bank buys an item for a client and the client agrees to pay the bank the price and a pre agreed profit later on.

b) Leasing- here the bank buys an item for the client and then gives on lease to him for a decided period and after completion of the period the lessee is supposed to pay the balance on the price decided in the beginning and then becomes the owner of the item.

c) Hire-purchase- here the bank buys an item for the client and then hires it for a decided rent and period, and at the completion of the period the client automatically becomes the owner of the item.

d) Sell-and-buy-back- here the client sells his property to the bank for an agreed amount which is payable now on this condition that the client will buyback the property after certain time at an agreed price.

e) Letters of credit- here the bank imports the item for the client on this basis that when the item is sold the bank will share the profits from the sale or on a mark-up basis.

4. Lending

There are three types of lending which are as follows:

a) Banks give loan without interest but cover their expenses by charging for its services in the form of service charges. This charge is set as per the subject to a maximum as per authorities.

b) No- cost Loans or Qard Hassan or benevolent loans: Here the banks set aside some funds to grant loans without any costs to help needy people like small farmers, small business men, small producers, etc. and to some needy consumers.

c) Overdrafts are to be provided, subject to a certain maximum limit, which is free of charge.

5. Services

Other banking services like bill collections, money transfers, trade in foreign currencies at spot rate etc. in which the bank's own money is not involved are rendered on a commission or charges basis.

It is important to understand the rationale of interest free banking in context of India.

1.3 Rationale for Zero Interest Based Banking in India

It is clear from the above activities performed by Zero Interest based Banks that they have a clear avoidance of interest which distinct itself from its contemporary conventional banking system where the major source of income is interest. But with this difference also Zero Interest based Banking has become a buzzword all over the world as it is a fairer banking system and is considered less risky too. It is interesting to find that Zero Interest based Banking is growing at a tremendous rate all over the world but still a large part of market is untapped especially in a country like India where Muslim population is the world's third largest.

This indeed is a very important reason that Zero Interest based Banking should come to India. Something which is very interesting to note is that, most of the Muslims in India are using traditional banking as they do not have any other option but still they are doing away with interest by giving the amount of interest as charity, so they are modifying the Indian banking system as per their convenience to lead their lives as per Sharia, because of this reason only Muslims are investing majorly in equity of those companies which are functioning on halal (permissible) terms or which are not involved in the business of alcohol, interest, etc. Muslims are also not saving money by investing in Fixed Deposits, PPF, etc as they give interest onto savings. So Muslims are paying all the taxes almost in full of the incomes which they are earning in India. Thus it can be said that a Muslim does not evade taxes by investing his money in interest laden schemes for tax savings. Another very strong reason which advocates for Interest free banking in India is that, there is a large number of Muslim population which cannot get access to bank loans and thus have a handicap in starting up a business, or taking up an educational loan, auto loan, etc.

An insight on various philosophies is important at this point to understand the mechanism of interest in the economy.

1.4 Philosophies on Interest

The Greek philosopher, Aristotle, condemned acquiring of wealth by the practice of charging of interest on money.

"Very much disliked also is the practice of charging interest: and the dislike is fully justified for interest is a yield arising out of money itself, not a product of that for which money was provided. Money was intended to be a means of exchange; interest represents an increase in the money itself. Hence of all ways of getting wealth, this is the most contrary to nature." (Aristotle, The Politics, Penguin, 1995)

"Do not charge your brother interest, whether on money or food or anything else that may earn interest." (Deuteronomy 23:19)

"If you lend money to My people, to the poor among you, you are not to act as a creditor to him; you shall not charge him interest." The Holy Bible

"If you have money, do not lend it at interest, but give it to one from whom you will not get it back." (Gospel St Thomas, V95).

It is just not disliked as it is in the religious books of people but also due to the fact that interest creates instability in the economy and by creating a gap between rich and the poor and with interest this gap becomes wider. These consequences have been highlighted by Mills (1993) as follows:

1. The unfair and destabilized distribution of returns among the users and suppliers of finance.
2. The unfair allocation of finances to the safest borrowers rather than the most productive ones
3. A tendency to finance speculation in assets and property.
4. An intrinsically unstable banking system which can only continue to exist with government guarantees.
5. A short term investment strategy.
6. The wealth being confined to fewer hands.
7. A rapid flow of financial capital across regions and countries where returns can be seen. Economic theory may believe that this will advance the efficiency of investment, but it contribute to the erosion of community and regional structure as jobs and opportunities have a propensity to follow flows of financial capital and thus can result in mass migrations.

So it is not only that Islam suggests that an interest free economy is more ethical and just, but also Christianity and Jewish followers also have a similar thought about interest and thus there is no wonder that Zero Interest based banking is being widely accepted by other than Muslims as well. It is important to study and analyse the different models, concepts and notions which can be implemented in a country like India.

1.5 Zero Interest Based Banking and Development

Zero Interest based banks provide such financial services which are as per the Sharia that is Islamic law, so if the Zero Interest based banks can procure the Muslim population it can result in hastening the economic development of the developing countries. It can be seen from the performance of Islamic banks that there is a double-digit expansion for a decade and Islamic banks has become an increasingly viable alternative to commercial banks in Islamic countries and the countries which have good number of Muslim populations.

Knowing what drives the progress of Zero Interest based banking it will help in development of countries in Asia, Africa and the Middle East. In its initial stages, Zero Interest based banking required much interpretation of Shariah law by Islamic scholars. In the earlier years, the basic implementation guidelines such as legislation as per which such banks are allowed to be set up and the training of staff was the main factors responsible for the reach of Zero Interest based banking. And in the past few years there has been a more improved regulation of liquidity and management accounting and rapid innovation.

In a similar way, the sukuk (Islamic bonds) has brought a revolution in Sharia finance in recent years as Islam prohibits interest bearing bonds. By using sophisticated financial techniques sukuk has become a multibillion dollar industry. In the Gulf interest free banks, in terms of their assets has one quarter of the industry and has share in single digits elsewhere.

Fig. 1.1 Share of Islamic Banks and Conventional Banks

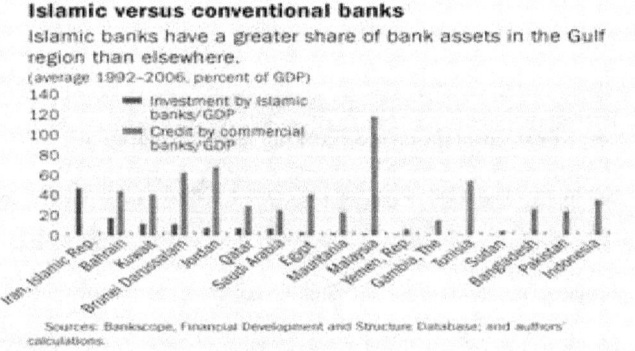

Source: www.imf.org

1.6 Interest Free Banking and Recession

While analyzing recession in terms of its causes, it can be consumer debt, low consumer confidence, inflation, over-valuation of assets, large scale unemployment and the most crucial of all that is high interest rates that can lead to an economic recession.

The cause of recession was the advancement of loans by the banks to people who are not very strong financially. These loans were later converted into bonds and sold to the investors in open market. Later, when the interest rates hiked, repayment of loans became difficult for the people and the loans were defaulted. Hence, the investors lost their money and ultimately the banks crashed and its aftermath was recession. The Federal Reserve could not reduce interest rates and the condition perpetually deteriorated. Therefore, interest was the major reason of the recession. The countries which remain less affected by recession were those which were practicing Zero Interest based Banking like Iran.

"Iran's banks were somewhat insulated from the global financial turmoil affecting the developed world. Although profits across the sector remained relatively static in The Banker's Top 1000 listings this year, a boom in Islamic financing has added much-needed ballast to banks' bottom lines. Iranian banks now hold $235bn of sharia-compliant assets, which makes up 37.5% of total sharia-compliant assets worldwide." (www.thebanker.com, 2009)

In the light of the above developments of Islamic banking worldwide, it is important to understand the possibility of Islamic banking or Zero interest based banking or Interest free banking in India.

1.7 Interest Free Banking: Possibility in India

It is apparent that the traditional banking system had its limitations and is being recognised all over the world thus, it is important to study and analyse the interest free system of banking in India and attempts have to be made to execute the models and concepts given by different authors with respect to IFB. For this purpose two such models are being discussed below by Gafoor (2005) and Shingeri (2007).

Gafoor (2005) mentioned that commercial banking operations are entirely interest based and receiving and lending on interest is prohibited in Islam. As interest is infused in all the operations of commercial banking system thus the whole banking system is not acceptable by Muslims. Yet as per Gafoor (2005) they cannot do without it, in a country where there is no other option. Thus, there are efforts to search for a banking system which is without interest. But the question arises, that if the element of interest is removed from the commercial banking system, will it be as good as the system people are accustomed to.

To remove the element of interest from the commercial banking system it must be understood the exact role of interest in the system. Then only removing it from the current system and its effects can be considered and thereby its viability can be examined.

Gafoor (2005) has explained the commercial banking system first and then eliminated the interest factor and devised a model which is as good as commercial banking sans interest which seems applicable in a country like India, which has only one kind of banking system and there are a lot of people who are in a fix in such a system who are interest averse. With the following examples it can be clear how interest can be eliminated from the present banking system to make it interest free.

Suppose person A has to start a new business and he needs capital for the same, he will ask his friends who can provide the credit to him. So he will call them and ask for credit and ask for some days to return the same. Let's assume that his friends are residing in different places and all agreed to give him credit for say a year then he has to get the money for that he has to travel to those places and communicate and finally get all the amount and start with his business the moment he starts making money he starts returning money in instalments to the people whom he owed the sum and finally he is able to pay all the amount he had borrowed say after a year.

This is a very simple example where Mr. A knew his friends but as everyone is not so lucky as Mr. A so they have to hire someone who knows such people who have wealth and can lend with some return, here the function of bank comes wherein the people who have their money with the bank act as lenders and people who need money approach the bank and it acts as a mediator between the two.

As Mr. A had to travel and communicate and for all this he must have incurred certain expenses so the same expenses are being charged by the bank in the form of disbursement charges so the same can be continued as interest is not involved.

This was a simple example of a simple loan wherein it can be safely concluded that a bank can function as a creditor which does not take any interest for disbursing a loan and also end up earning a fee which is for disbursement of loan, making the money available to the debtor and taking care of funds which is available with the bank and for mitigating the risk involved. In the entire process they can also charge or put up a fee for accounting inflation in the process. So the bank can also earn an income without involving interest in this scenario. Such and more of these kinds of transactions can take place which can make the present banking system as interest free banking system.

Now the question arises, that people who deposit money with the banks will they be able to earn as they used to earn interest with the savings account? The answer is yes they can also earn if the bank earns a profit the same can be distributed to the people who are keeping their money with the bank. So this can be safely concluded that if the people who are keeping money with the banks do not earn interest then the banks can function without interest in imparting loans.

The following is the discussion on a system which is apparently commercial but can be made interest free as explained by Gafoor (2005) by comparing the model of cost in the present system and how it can be replaced or how can interest be removed from the present system:

Cost of Borrowing

In the present Commercial Banking system the CoB can be broken down into: interest, cost of services, cost of overheads, risk premium, profit (remuneration to the bank), and compensation of value depreciation caused by inflation.

Cost of borrowing (CoB) = Interest+ Cost of Services+ Cost of Overheads+ Risk Premium+ Profit+ Compensation for Inflation

This is the model of a typical commercial bank now we should analyse the components one by one and find out whether they can be continued or dropped in our interest free commercial banking.

Interest- It is the fixed amount which the bank pays to the depositors of the bank who keep their money with the bank in the form of time deposits and savings deposits. This component of CoB is prohibited and is called Riba in Islam and should be dropped from our model.

Services Cost- This is the actual cost of providing services for a transaction which may include legal and other charges paid for title, preparation of loan documents, evaluation of collateral, etc. This may vary from transaction to transaction but do not depend on the duration and size of the loan. Thus it does not fall into the prohibited category and has no resemblance to interest.

Overheads and other services- There are some other services which are provided to the borrower directly or indirectly apart from the service cost mentioned above like:

Services to the borrowers: Maintenance of the borrower's account, problem solving, correspondence, etc. As a client of the bank he holds a current account and receives transaction services (deposits, withdrawals, cheque transfers, etc.) The volume of these services increases with a new borrowing and depends on the size and duration of the loan.

Services to the depositors- the bank have mainly two kinds of depositors' savings account holders and current account holders and they are the accounts from where the bank raises funds. The more and the better these services are provided the more number of depositors will be attracted for more funds to lend.

Advertisements- So for increasing more funds, the bank needs to go for advertising and educating the people to deposit their money with the bank for safety and growth and thus has to bear the cost of advertising and educating people.

Overheads cost- This includes office rent, staff salaries and general administration costs as well as the overall maintenance o the bank like bank buildings, equipment, materials and stationery, postage, etc.

All the above services provided and costs incurred to bring more funds to enable more loans to be advanced thus these costs are passed on to the borrower.

Risk premium

In commercial banking loans are granted as per collateral. The bank has recourse to the collateral in case of default. Yet defaults, delays, frauds, etc are common. Thus bank has to take preventive measures and the cost of such measures again has to be borne by the users of the bank's funds.

This can be achieved by creating a collective default insurance scheme. This needs to be proportional to the amount involved. Any loss the bank incurs due to bad loans can be made good by this fund. This risk premium is a fully or partially refundable "deposit" which will make all loans considerably cheaper.

Profit

The components which we have discussed so far are all costs (expenses), which the bank incurs but they are not earning anything extra just covering their costs but they should be remunerated for their contribution, which is actually profit. It should be charged to the customer. The profit can be charged by fixing a percentage of services and overhead costs, increase these costs accordingly, and call them services charge and overheads charge respectively.

Inflation

Inflation affects the CoB in two ways: by affecting the cost of services, overheads the capital and by eroding the value of the capital. We assume a zero inflation which will have no effect on the CoB. Now we will examine some situations to find out whether they fall under the prohibited category or not.

Lending by individuals- if an individual takes money from another and gives additional amount at the time of payment assuming inflation to be zero, no risk, no services cost, no overheads costs and as there is no cost involved so profit component becomes zero. Here the additional amount the borrower is paying is interest.

Bank lending from time and savings deposits- This dealing has interest in it, thus prohibited.

Lending by individuals- if they are not asking for any return then it's not interest and only asking for the expenses they have incurred in providing this money then obviously this has to be borne which is an everyday situation and does not involve interest.

Current Account deposits- Most of the banks do not pay interest to current account deposit holders, thus it is free of interest.

Government lending through banks- Suppose Government deposits money with commercial banks to induce growth of private sector and asks banks to grant loans to suitable entrepreneurs at "a reduced rate of interest". The Government requires the principal be paid back but nothing more. As here the depositor is not asking for the money so the so called "interest" is actually the amount of other components of CoB which the bank has to bear and being transferred to the borrower. This situation is actually free of interest.

Other banking services- Money transfer, sale and purchase of foreign currency generally do not require any advance of funds by the bank. Only a fee is charged for the service. Hence there is no interest component in these transactions.

From the above discussion and analysis it can be concluded that the depositor with the bank is actually lending the money to the borrower through the bank and as long as he does not demand any return for his money the entire system can be made interest free. Obviously the question arises, that why people will keep money with the bank when they do not get anything in return so the simple answer to this is as interest is prohibited in Islam so people can avoid it as they do not lose anything and they are guaranteed their capital and by dropping the component of interest the new cost of borrowing is like this.

Cost of Borrowing (CoB) = Cost of Services+ Cost of Overheads+ Risk Premium+ Profit+ Compensation for Inflation

The above model if applied in the present banking system will have no complications as it does not require any changes in the legal system but it does require some efforts from the banks so that they may take steps for its implementation.

Another model given by Shingeri (2007) on which a company named "al Taqwa Finances PLC" in Karnataka is based and is being run to do a feasibility study.

Kinds of accounts in Interest Free Bank (IFB)

Demand Credit a/c is like a current account and Time Credit A/c is for fostering economic development of the weaker sections of the community, it seeks to mobilize the idle savings of the upper strata by way of accepting time credits which can be withdrawn at the expiry of the agreed period.

Time Credit a/c holders cannot demand money before maturity and put up with the terms and conditions of the bank and if they require money they can be given loan on their deposit as loan against deposit.

For liquidation of debts (if any) the IFB has following options:

1. It will use its reserve with the central bank to meet the immediate requirements.

2. It will absorb the loss in its profit

3. The shareholders will be called upon to increase their shareholding

Fig. 1.2 Types of Accounts in IFB

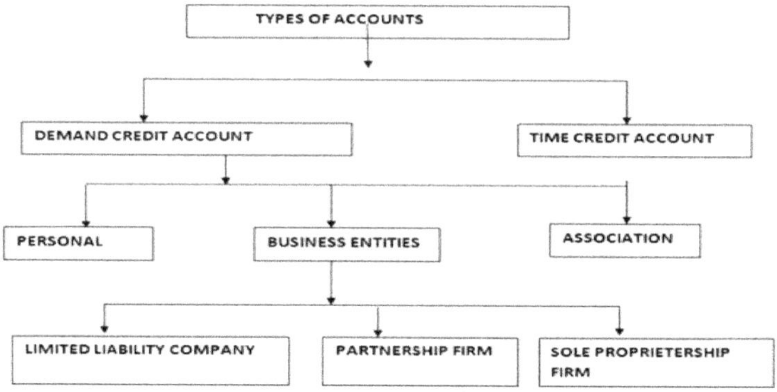

```
                        TYPES OF ACCOUNTS
                               |
              -----------------------------------
              |                                 |
     DEMAND CREDIT ACCOUNT              TIME CREDIT ACCOUNT
              |
   -------------------------------
   |              |              |
PERSONAL   BUSINESS ENTITIES  ASSOCIATION
                  |
      ----------------------------------
      |              |                 |
LIMITED LIABILITY  PARTNERSHIP   SOLE PROPRIETORSHIP
    COMPANY           FIRM              FIRM
```

Source: Shingeri (2007)

Term Investment Account

This account comprises of investment of a specific amount of money invested with the IFB by any one, such as individuals, industrialists, business entities, etc for a fixed period of time (minimum a week). The investment can be withdrawn after the maturity period only. The percentage of profit will be fixed during the account opening negotiations between the investors and the IFB. The investment will be based on the principles of Mudaraba. Mudaraba is an agreement between two parties for a joint venture in which one party provides finance called investor (RabAl–Maal) and the other party who puts in time and services called active partner or working partner as Mudarib. The percentage of income has to be fixed beforehand.

In the Mudaraba agreement the working partner gets to have a share in the profits but the losses are borne by the investor as in the event of loss the investor loses money and the working partner loses his time and remuneration. The investor has the right to investigate the causes of loss through appointment of an Audit Firm or a Zero Interest based Judicial Committee.

Share Capital/Sponsor's Shares-

The IFB will call for shares from public who will be required to fill in an application form prescribed by the IFB. The applicants need not make prepayments immediately as they will be called upon to do so, only when they are selected by the IFB. Such shareholders' liability will be limited upon the paid up portion of the shares. The IFB's capital will also comprise of sponsors' shares or founder's shares, whose liabilities will also be limited to their shares.

The sponsor's shares will be run on account of Shariah principle **Musharakah** which is a type of business setup, where two or more persons or institutions, invest their capital jointly in such a way that the return thus realized, is distributed between them.

Investments

The IFB will adopt four modes of investments in the initial stages to utilize the funds raised from its customers, public shares and sponsor's shares as:

Fig. 1.3 Types of Investments

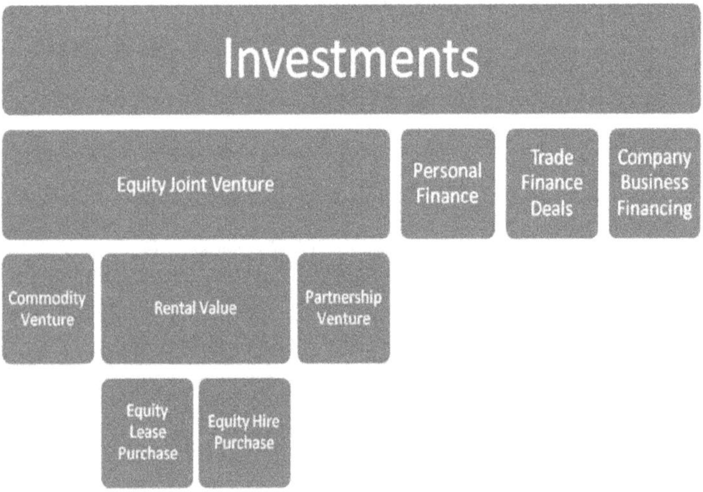

```
                        Investments
   ┌──────────────────────────────┬───────────┬──────────┬──────────┐
   │     Equity Joint Venture     │ Personal  │  Trade   │ Company  │
   │                              │ Finance   │ Finance  │ Business │
   │                              │           │ Deals    │Financing │
   └──────────────────────────────┴───────────┴──────────┴──────────┘
   ┌───────────┬─────────────┬─────────────┐
   │ Commodity │ Rental Value│ Partnership │
   │  Venture  │             │   Venture   │
   └───────────┴─────────────┴─────────────┘
               ┌──────────┬──────────┐
               │  Equity  │  Equity  │
               │  Lease   │   Hire   │
               │ Purchase │ Purchase │
               └──────────┴──────────┘
```

Source: Shingeri (2007)

Equity Joint Venture

Equity joint venture is a major process of investment in the financing scheme of the IFB. The main objectives of this scheme are:

1) To extend its facility to all types of industrial or commercial entrepreneurs according to the nature of their businesses.
2) To encourage technical assistance services.

The IFB will grant the following facilities depending on the needs:

(a) Commodity Venture

The major purpose of this facility is to provide financial assistance to entrepreneurs who may need funds to purchase merchandise for trading. This facility operates on the basis of **Murabaha** in which the IFB will buy the merchandise needed and sell it to the client with a higher price keeping a mark up which is IFB's profit.

(b) Rental Venture- The venture will be operated on the Sharia principle "**Ijarah**". It is a contract for the use of rental assets or properties (tangible or intangible) for a specified period of time, at a fixed rent". The IFB has divided the rental venture into two subcategories

(i) Equity lease purchase

(ii) Equity hire purchase

(i) Equity lease purchase- in this case the lessee will obtain the asset on a lease basis and has to pay rent for it and the ownership remains with the IFB. At the end of lease the lessee has the option to either purchase the asset at the depreciated value or not. If the lessee purchases it at the depreciated value that will be the profit of the IFB and if it does not then IFB can sell it at the market value and earn profit thereupon. In case of the default the asset will be confiscated by the IFB and sold in the market.

(ii) Equity Hire Purchase- in this contract the IFB will provide its prospective customer with a facility to purchase on installment basis, an asset of variable nature (whose market value keeps fluctuating) such as land, houses, shops and factories, etc. The client will be able to take possession of the asset on rent, as soon as the contract is signed.

(c) Partnership Venture- The IFB under this venture will grant finance to selected skilled clients who wish to establish some projects with financial assistance of the IFB. The grant of such assistance will be on the principles of **Mudarabah** or **Musharakah**.

As in a country like India it is not allowed for a bank to get into partnership with the client thus it cannot be adopted in such countries.

(I) Personal Finance- the IFB will extend its financial services to individuals as well. This will be done to assist its clients in purchasing consumer goods such as items of luxury, comfort, or of basic necessity, either on the principle of Ijarah or Murabaha.

(II) Trade Finance Deal- The trade finance deal is a scheme of financing customers for trading – in spot commercial transactions. It involves two contracts:

(i) The Purchase Commitment contract

(ii) The Sale Commitment Contract

(III) Company Business Financing- this scheme will be operated on the Shariah principle called **Musharakah**, which is a type of business setup, where two or more persons or institutions, invest their capital jointly in such a way that the return thus realized, is distributed between them.

This scheme will be available to running and well established active business organization requiring finance for the growth of their business either in the form of expansion or diversification into new activities or meeting their cash requirements to meet their commitments.

By having an understanding of the above interest free banking models it can be understood that the present commercial banking system can be made interest free adopting the practices of Islamic banking and by making certain changes in the present banking system. At this point, it is important to know about wealth creation through Islamic banking.

1.8 Value Creation in Interest free Banking

A rapid expansion of Islamic banking in Muslim countries and non Muslim countries like United Kingdom, Australia, China, and Hong Kong is a significant development in this century. The major difference of Zero Interest based banking from the commercial banking system is basically the avoidance of interest that is riba and promotion of profit and loss sharing concept. Zero Interest based banks have an array of transactions mostly based on Profit and Loss Sharing System that could be appealing for a range of clientele. These are inclusive of two major methods of financing, mudarabah and musharakah, is allowed as per Sharia because profit/loss and risk are shared evenly between the parties in the contract.

By offering mudarabah and musharakah, the Zero Interest based banking system encourages social and economic fairness by creating such an environment which promotes co-operation and harmony in the society.

The implementation of Profit and Loss Sharing (PLS) modes of financing by Zero Interest based banks act as intermediaries which results in fairness by facilitating the interests of the community as a whole and is expected to encourage increase in value to depositors and shareholders and consequently, to the economy as a whole. Interest based instruments basically favour the rich and works against the interests of the common people which is not the case with a PLS system.

Commercial Banks usually prefer to grant loan money to those who have money as they are able to pay their interests and other such charges. When the entrepreneurs borrow money from banks they use the depositor's money for funding of their own projects. In the earnings of profit they do not have to pay anything to the depositors. Losses in their projects may lead to bankruptcy of the bank itself, and will be passed on to the depositors who will have to bear the losses and thus interest based system creates inequity and imbalance in the distribution of wealth amongst the people in the economy.

In PLS depositors and entrepreneurs are willing to share the result of the project in an equal way. If there is a profit it will be shared between them at a pre arranged proportions and if there is a loss, all financial losses are borne by the one who is providing capital (the Zero Interest based Bank) and the loss of labour has to be borne by the entrepreneur also known as mudarib in the practice of Mudarabah arrangement. This can be useful in building the bridge between the capital providers and budding entrepreneurs who have business skills but lack capital. PLS financing can also encourage economic growth by giving the opportunities by funding skilled entrepreneurs.

As per Matthews, Tlemsani and Siddique (2004), the economic principles of Zero Interest based finance of sharing risks and rewards, involvement in creation of wealth through equity financing by entrepreneurs and investors, has a potential to increase creativity and output in the economy. Additionally PLS agreements promote fairness and value creation for all the contracting parties alike.

Though, there have been experiences as discussed by (Abalkhail and Presley, 2000; Ahmed, 2002) that there could be some unavoidable issues like moral hazard, asymmetric information and adverse selection which can hinder the implementation of the PLS system. In spite of the above issues (Ismail et al. 2014) proposed Zero Interest based banking for its value addition in the economic system and also suggested that Zero Interest based banks need to develop a combination of mark-up modes and profit sharing modes of financing.

It can be understood by the above studies that adoption of Zero Interest based banking can lead to value creation for not only the Islamic banks but also all the stakeholders associated with it be it customers, shareholders or the economy as a whole. It can drive the entire financial system to a different motive which is to create equilibrium between social and substantial objectives to provide fairness and social justice. Though, the success of the PLS model in financial system is dependent on the resolution of the imperfections which can occur in their use.

1.9 Objectives of the Study

The objectives of the study are:

- To explore the level of awareness of Islamic banking amongst different sections of the society in India.
- To discover the impact of level of education on the preference of Islamic banking i.e. Islamic banking methods.
- To observe the attitude of people towards adoption of Islamic or Interest free bank in India.
- To compare the application of Islamic banking methods with other methods in India.
- To analyze the possibilities of Islamic banking in India.

- To analyze the behavior of Muslim population in India in using the interest which they receive from commercial banks and also to analyze whether they are investing in interest laden schemes for investment.
- To study the legal framework within which an Islamic bank can exist in India.
- To observe and examine the challenges of interest free banking in India.

1.10 Hypotheses of the Study

On the basis of the objectives and the research questions to be answered for the study, following hypotheses have been formulated:

- H_{01}: There is no significant difference in awareness Sharia banking amongst Muslims and non Muslims.
- H_{02}: There is no dissimilarities of education level over preference of interest free methods of banking.
- H_{03}: There is no difference in application of Islamic banking methods among Muslims and Non Muslims.
- H_{A4}: Muslims are taking measures to avoid interest by not investing in interest laden schemes.
- H_{A5}: Muslims are giving in charity the interest which they receive from banks.
- H_{06}: There is no difference in getting affected by motivating factors of Sharia Islamic Banking in India amongst Muslims and Non Muslim customers.

1.11 Scope of the Study

The present research has been conducted to explore the possibilities of Islamic banking in India through a survey of people who are using the conventional banking system. This will give a picture of the prospective demand of Islamic Banking in India, their issues with the present conventional banking system, their steps and measures to avoid interest in their day to day financial transactions. The type of sampling used for this study is convenience sampling in different parts of the country.

1.12 Research Approach

A rational research approach is required for the validity of any social research. In order to test the awareness, preferences, willingness, perception, opinion of people towards Sharia banking system a survey was conducted on respondents in NCT of Delhi. The research methodology adopted in the completion of the study has been discussed in detail in chapter 2 of this study.

1.13 Limitations of the Study

The study is confined to a sample of 311 persons from different religious groups in India considering the awareness of Sharia financial system in Islam which is at very low level even among the population following Islam. The sample population of this study has been drawn from Delhi and NCR. The findings of this study have been generalized with certain observations. The legal framework for banking industry in India is interest based, therefore the possibility of introducing zero interest banking require additional/amended laws.

It is after introduction to the concept of interest free banking, its possibilities in India, objectives, hypotheses and limitations of the study in the present chapter, the review of literature and research methodology used to conduct the present study are discussed in next chapter.

CHAPTER-2

LITERATURE REVIEW AND RESEARCH METHODOLOGY

The present chapter is devoted to the review of literature on the subject and the research methodology adopted to complete the present study.

2.1 Literature Review

One of the most significant objectives of the thesis is to find out the prospects of Sharia banking system in India. Particularly, it aims to discover the level and magnitude of awareness of the various terminologies of Islamic banking system and Islamic methods of financing and investments, the influence of motivating factors, attitude of respondents towards Islamic methods of finance, their thought on implementation of Islamic Banking, and their application of Interest free Banking in their financial day to day transactions. The objective of the chapter is to present reviewed literature related to the customer's perception and outlook towards the Islamic methods of financing and investment.

This chapter contains the following four sections.

1. General studies of Islamic banking
2. Studies related to awareness and attitude towards Islamic banking.
3. Studies related to the need, scope, growth potential, practicability and prospects of the Sharia banking in India.
4. Studies in support of Islamic banking.

After reviewing the literature available from different sources, the researcher got acquainted with the theoretical aspects of Islamic finance and banking which helped in the identification of the research gap.

2.1.1 General Studies on Islamic Banking

(Qureshi 1946) suggested that the banks should be seen as social service sponsored by government as public health and education, as the Sharia banking institutions neither can pay any interest nor charge even a single penny in the form of interest, and has also given an alternative of partnerships between banks and businessmen, sharing losses if any, not mentioning anything about profit sharing.

Ahmad (1952): Ahmad authored a book titled as 'Economics of Islam', visualized the establishing of Sharia banking institutions by forming a company with limited liability. An opportunity may be provided for opening an account somewhat like current accounts upon which no commission is paid or charged for depositing and borrowing fund through these accounts respectively. However there may be an account through which investors may invest or deposit their funds on partnership basis in return of dividends, generated by investment of these funds. Besides Ahmad predicted about the possible partnership arrangement with the owner of the business who seeks finance from the banking institutions. But he did not discussed about the proportion of profits or losses to be shared by both parties to the transactions.

Scholars have also justified banning of interest by giving economic reasons as interest is a prearranged fee or charge of manufacturing or production which thwarts full employment. (Khan 1968; Mannan 1970).

Mohsin (1982) elaborated on to the coexistence of Islamic banks with conventional banks also suggested as the Islamic banking business has to survive without interest so it has to perform host of financial services like trust business, factoring, real estate, consultancy. Though these financial services are highly specialised, it may be futile for most of the nations in the Arab world in the contemporary stage of growth and development. It can be useful in the capitalist economy thus indicating the coexistence.

Siddiqi (1968): one of the most pioneering attempts made in order to provide a detailed sketch of Sharia based banking system was made by Siddiqi in the year 1968. He has authored his work on Sharia based banking system in the Urdu language. The Sharia based banking system model developed by the researcher draws upon the principles of Mudarba and Shrikun (partnership or musharaka as it is now usually called).This model was basically constructed on a dualistic principle, Mudaraba sponsor and entrepreneur association, apart from this he did efforts in describing the mechanism of such transactions as detailed as possible with abundant imaginary and reckoning examples. He categorised business activities of Sharia based banking institutions into these three major categories: firstly, the banking services which are based on fees, commissions or other fixed charges; second, financing activities based on the principle of Mudaraba and partnership; and the third is financial services which are provided free of costs or commissions. In his research work the researcher proposed that Sharia based interest-free banking institutions could be proved as a viable substitute to the traditional and interest-based banking establishments.

Ariff (1982) contested that interest has been proved a least effective economic strategy instrument and hence is not considered an effective determining factor of savings and investments activities.

There have been a lot of literature available in Urdu and Arabic about Islamic banking, and a brief discussion of such literature is found in the book 'Banking without Interest' by Nejatullah Siddiqi (1983)

Chapra (1985) pointed out the Islamic Banking system as not only abolition of interest based banking system but also its contribution and role in promoting social welfare oriented schemes and business projects rather than a profit maximizing role. The author suggested that Islamic banking institutions must focus on serving the interest of public rather than focussing or emphasising on individual interests and also emphasized the urgency to form an organisation that will assist in setting regulatory framework as well as an agenda in order to oversee Sharia financial institutions. Besides they further mentioned that training of Sharia banking and financial regulatory authorities and supervisors for better internal rating and controlling system for reducing risk. This will result into improved external performance of the Sharia banks as well as would help them in capitalizing their equity funds more efficiently with increased growth and stability. Besides they explained few significant judicial issues that need to be solved to facilitate the better supervision of Sharia banking institutions and accelerate their growth rate. It also calls for facilities and assistance that are required to be provided to help these banks in order to overcome various issues and problems faced by them.

Few case studies on Sharia based or Islamic banking institutions have been conducted in Bangladesh also (Huq 1986), Egypt (Mohammad 1986), Malaysia (Halim 1988b), Pakistan (Khan 1986), Sudan (Salama 1988b) etc. Almost all of these studies disclosed thought-provoking resemblances and differences. In all these banks, the study of the current accounts revealed that in all respondent banks the current accounts are operated on the principles of alwadiah. While the study about Savings deposits accounts disclosed, that these too, are accepted on the alwadiah basis, but gifts to the investors or depositors are agreed completely at the choice of the Islamic banking organisations on the minimum balance, so that the depositors can also have a share in profits of the investment done through these type of funds principle of Mudaraba, but there are substantial discrepancies. For example, the Islamic Bank of Bangladesh offers PLS Deposit Accounts, PLS Special Notice Deposit Accounts and PLS Term Deposit Accounts, while on the other hand the Islamic bank of Malaysia use to offer two types of investment deposit accounts, one for the public in general such as individual depositors and the second is for institutional investors or customers.

Though the concept of Islamic banking was there at the reign of Muhammad (Pbuh) the last messenger of Islam. As per Islamic belief system, the first official Islamic Banking transaction was conducted at Mit Ghamr in Egypt in late 1963; Islamic banking system is a pool of financing as well as investment activities according to the Sharia i.e. law of Islam. As per Islam the followers are prohibited from accepting and paying any interest, henceforth they find it quite difficult to do business transactions with commercial banks. Gerrard and Cunningham (1997)

Alam(2000)conducted a comparative study of Islamic Banking practices of an interest free financial institution named as Islamic Bank Bangladesh Limited (IBBL) with conventional banking practices, also highlighted the contribution of Islamic banks towards small and rural section. The author has shown how interest free banks perform along with the conventional banks in the country; he has also elaborated detailed accounts of its financial activities in the country since the inception of Sharia banking system in the country.

Bagsiraj (2003) in his study found out that there are around 300 Sharia based banking institutions but there is a paucity of information regarding their business activities, financial performance, future prospects etc. He categorised these banking organisations in four groups such as; Islamic financial societies (IFSs), Islamic co-operative credit societies (ICCSs), Islamic investment and financial companies (IIFCs), and financial association of persons (FAPs).

Vasu (2005) studied the interest free mechanism as one of the basic characteristics of Islamic financial system. Though banking activities such as investment and financing in the absence of interest rate system are perceived to be an illusion because it is quite difficult to believe lending and borrowing of funds without any interest, but despite this, the concept of interest free banking and financial system is getting popular day by day in the world both in the Arab countries as well as other nations of the world and the author is of the opinion that in future Sharia based banking practices may also be accommodated in the Indian banking industry. The author also suggested the viability of Islamic Banking in India seeing the success in different Muslim and Non Muslim countries.

Tripathy (2009) mentioned that Muslims comprise of 15% of the population in India but their account holding in 27 public sector banks is only 12%. The priority sector lending by 29 Private sector banks is held by 11% of Muslims in India. Thus the government of India is showing interest in Sharia compliant banking, which has gained support from some political parties. Sharia based banking and financial undertakings may appeal more Muslim investors and borrowers to the organized banking system and will help in community's development.

Haque, Lone and Thakur (2010) deployed SWOT analysis and Michael Porter's five point models to explain the sustainability of Islamic financial practices in India. They advocated Islamic Bank of Britain, Islamic banks of Thailand, Singapore and USA as brilliant examples to initiate Islamic banking practices in the India. It was advocated that the renowned national as well as international banks along with Reserve Bank of India must participate in the process of determination and execution of Islamic financial products in India. They referred "Islamic Banking" synonymous to "Interest Free Banking" so that it may be perceived rather through a broad economic perspective than a narrow religious prism.

A study by Manzoor Khalidi and Amanullah (2010) for the perception of customers about Islamic banks in 100 customers of Pakistan by using Z test showed that the customers are well aware of Sharia based banking system, though there was doubt about authenticity of the Sharia compliance of the Sharia banking practices and financial services while the religion had low priority for the choice of the bank.

Redimerio and Andrew (2011) reported, "Growing and deepening market for Islamic financing is a key reason why the Islamic finance market is worth to consider for the infrastructure sector. Infrastructure projects are a logical fit for Islamic finance, which is governed by Shariah and predicted on asset backing and shared business risk. Collateral security of assets in Sharia based financial system is rather better for infrastructural projects than traditional lenders operating on the basis of interest.

Sehrish Rustam et al.(2011) did a study on a random sample of 60 corporate customers of six Pakistani Islamic banks which had only Muslims as respondents, 55% expressed their willingness on introducing the Sharia based banking system as a substitute for interest based banking practices. 68% of the people surveyed felt that Islamic banks as well as interest based banking institutions both must aim for maximization of profits in order to survive in the competitive market. Besides 63.3% of the respondents interviewed indicated religion and economic benefits as two main determining factors to choose Islamic banking.

Malik,A., Malik, M.S. and Shah, H., (2011) highlighted the unexpected growth in the UK and the factors responsible for it. The unmatched support from the government, fastest growing Muslim population, and the incomes coming in from the Middle East were the major factors for the same. However, they mentioned the future seems very promising for the UK but it also has to face a set of challenges.

Rasheed, H., Amin, W. and Ahmed,A., (2012) compared Islamic banks in foreign and in Pakistan to find out the level of satisfaction and the factors and found that there is a positive correlation among the satisfaction derived by consumers and factors.

Abdul Aziz Abdullah, Sidek, R., and Adnan, A., (2012) conducted a research on the opinion of non Muslim people towards Sharia based Islamic banking institutions amid 152 clienteles of Kuwait Finance House. The outcome of this research revealed that Sharia based Islamic banking and financial services are going to be perceived by non Muslims positively and also concluded that Islamic banking system would be prevailing over the interest based conventional banking system in Malaysia in future.

Norma Md. Saad(2012) conducted a research about the client's contentment of Sharia based Islamic banks and Interest based traditional banks in Malaysia and the results of his study revealed that there is some association amid diverse demographic factors and the satisfaction level of banks clients among 1153 respondents, which showed that client satisfaction is dependent on the quality of services offered by these banking institutions.

Fada, K and Bundi Wabekwa (2012) in their research in Gombe Local Government Area (Nigeria) among 134 respondents revealed that Sharia based Islamic banks are more prevalent in youngsters and sophisticated people and a major portion of these people had known about Sharia based Islamic banking practices. 26.87% of the respondents had this notion that Islamic banking is only for Muslims. It was suggested that programs for increasing awareness should be done to educate people about it.

Urvi Amin (2012) conducted a research by deploying a non-probability sample of 100 respondents from the district of Ahmadabad (Gujarat) and its findings disclosed that

Muslim peoples in the selected sample did not seem to be very much persuaded towards the Sharia based principles of banking at the time of making investments but the most interesting thing is that they were interested in Islamic financial products at the time of financing decisions.

Emir Hidayat and Nouf K Al Bawardi (2013) conducted a study on 103 emigrant employees in the kingdom of Saudi Arabia, which comprises a major portion of Indian people to know the attitude of Non Muslims towards Islamic Banks and their practices in this study it was revealed that around 48% of the respondents preferred Islamic banking services as the service charges are less as compared to the traditional banking. They also concluded that the non Muslims customers find the Islamic banks are suitable and good enough in satiating their banking or financial requirements.

Similarly there is another research conducted by Shanmugam Muniswamy, Soundararajan, G. and Ramasamy, R., (2013). They surveyed around 150 teachers from 10 colleges in Chennai (Tamil Nadu), and concluded that there are noteworthy dissimilarities among Muslims and non-Muslims teachers about their readiness and their inclination to accept Islamic financial system.

2.1.2 Studies on Awareness and Attitude for Islamic Banking

Bley and Kuehn (2004) concentrated their research work on students' understanding and their opinions about Sharia based Islamic banking and financial institutions and their practices in an Arab nation named as United Arab Emirates (UAE). The sample was consisted of 676 students from Arab as well as non Arab nations. The findings of the study disclosed that a significant percentage of Muslim students preferred the Islamic banking products and facilities because of their religious sentiments and convictions. The second type of findings revealed that successful Arab Muslim peoples had very much understanding regarding the Sharia based Islamic financial banking services, terminologies and concepts and so on. While on the other hand, it was revealed through this study that affluent and prosperous non-Arab students were having a higher level of knowledge about interest based traditional banks and the financial services offered by them.

A research conducted in Adelaide Australia comprising of a sample of 300 Muslims by Rammal and Zurbruegg (2007) for their mindfulness of Sharia banking services showed that the significant portion of the population is inclined towards and ready to use Islamic banking practices for investment and financing purposes but they were having neither knowledge nor understanding about the operations and services of Islamic banks. While few of the surveyed respondents were having little understanding and exposure regarding the availability of Sharia financial institutions, their banking services, but despite this they were still ignorant about the fundamental Sharia based Islamic banking or financial principles and specific Islamic methods of financing business or other projects for example profit and or loss sharing contractual agreements. Also the lack of awareness of Muslims was not a hindrance in the enthusiasm of respondents to adopt Islamic methods of financing and investments. Respondents also revealed that adopting Islamic financial services was too contingent upon the variables such as the organization is of repute or not, availability of financial services and others which are incidental to main banking services for example facility of ATM, net banking, mobile banking and so on.

Khattak, N.A., and Kashifur Rehman (2010) tried to establish the correlation among demographic factors and contentment level and understanding of the clients of the about 156 people from various metropolises of Pakistan. The people surveyed revealed their satisfaction to a few of the devices or financial services and also dissatisfaction to a few, most of the banks clients were satisfied, they mostly had an understanding about the general products but unaware with the financial products like Mudarabah and Ijara.

Mark Loo (2010) conducted a study about the dissimilarities in outlook and discernment towards Sharia based Islamic banking system among people from the Islam religion and others by drawing a sample of around 200 people in Malaysia – 100 respondents were Muslim and 100 were non-Muslims at Klang valley (Malaysia) and revealed that Muslim people were compassionate about the Sharia based Islamic banking practices while on the other hand non-Muslims perceived Islamic banking system as useful and significant for the people who are from Muslim community.

Ahsanul Haque (2010) in a conversation with around 473 Malaysian clients studied the perceived discrepancies about Sharia banking services and in his research he came to know that there is a positive attitude towards the Sharia based Islamic banking system besides, he found that there are substantial attitudinal differences among Malay clients and Chinese clients, similarly amongst Chinese & Indian clients, while in the study it was found that all these three races were having positive opinion towards Sharia Islamic banking services. The findings of this research also revealed that a variable viz. gender (male and female) were also having a impact on the opinions of customers towards Sharia banking services.

Tambiah et al., (2011) did a comparison of urban and rural clients, both Muslims as well as non Muslims in Malaysia on cognizance, opinions and inclination of Sharia Retail Banking system. The results of this study revealed that people from both of these places posses mindfulness of Sharia based Islamic banking services but the unawareness was relatively higher among respondents from rural areas. In terms of complexities and risk rural respondents preferred Sharia Banking services to be more complex and ambiguous when paralleled with urban respondents. There was a difference between perception of Islamic banking among rural and urban customers. The views of respondent clients also differed in terms of income or returns raised from the fixed deposit accounts, various saving accounts or schemes, home loans with fixed maturity period, over draft services with minimal service charges with the opinion of urban respondents being more than that of rural respondents.

In a similar study, Nissar Ahmed Yatoo and S. Sudalai Muthu (2013) did an analysis of the impact of demographic factors such as age, gender, educational qualifications etc. on perception of clients towards Sharia banking services and this study primarily draws upon the primary data collected from 6 states in India and came to know that despite being a significant amount of growth in over 100 countries, Muslim people in India are not having understanding of the banking services of Sharia banking and finance. They suggested that there should be awareness campaigns to educate Muslims of India on the practice of Islamic banking.

Jamshidi D., Hussin, N. and Wan, H.L. (2013) studied the future implications of demographic variables on the use of Islamic banking services and established that Islamic banking system needs to attract new customers to sustain in the market and thus new and well formed strategies are needed for such a banking system. It is important to know the segmentation of the customers as per their preferences to provide customized services by the banks.

Yusuf and Shamsuddin (n.d) performed a study using purposive sampling on 128 respondents from Leicester U.K. to find out Muslims' attitude towards Islamic Banking living outside the Muslim world. They found that Muslims have a positive perception towards Sharia based banking services and are ready to forgo conventional banking for Islamic banking. Irrespective of their knowledge of Islamic banking 64% are ready to windup their present accounts and open a new one with the Islamic bank;

it was also found that education levels did not have any contribution in understanding of methods of Islamic finance.

As far as studies of the above nature with reference to Islamic banks are relatively new and therefore not much literature exist. Internationally various researches have been conducted in this field and one of the previous studies was conducted by Erol and El-Bdour(1989).

The study was carried out in Jordan and had a sample of 434 respondents to study the attitude, behaviour and benefaction factors of bank customers towards Islamic banking. It was revealed that the respondents had awareness of the Islamic banking services and that religion as motivating factor was not only the primary measure for the choice of Islamic banking services.

Though religious motivation was not completely absent in the respondents, they were profit oriented as they were used to the conventional interest based banking environment.

Omar (1992) did a study on 300 Muslims in the UK to show their selected benefaction variables and understanding towards Sharia techniques of finance. It was found that a high degree of unawareness existed amongst respondents about the principles of Islamic finance, it can be suggested that the awareness of Islamic methods of finance has differences among Muslim clients as per their country.

Norafifah Ahmad, Sudin Haron and Sandra L.Planisek (1994) did a research on 301 Muslim and Non Muslim clients of conventional banks in Malaysia to know about the bank preference factors by collecting data through self administered questionnaire. They did univariate and multivariate analysis. Muslims clients as well as and non Muslim clients have common preference factors in selection of the bank, thus it was advised by the author to the Islamic banks to focus on handling their customers and improvement in quality of services.

Gerrard and Cunningham (1997) studied the difference in degree of awareness and opinion between Muslims and non Muslims towards Islamic finance in Singapore using a questionnaire taking 190 respondents as the sample. They found that Muslims aware more knowledge about the terminology of Islamic financial services, but Muslims and non Muslims both were unaware of the Islamic financial terms. The study also showed that there is a difference in the attitude of Muslims and non Muslims towards Islamic banking. They concluded that there are significant differences in the ranking of the selection criteria between Muslims and non Muslims. As there was a lack of awareness of Islamic banking terms and practices it was suggested more efforts should be made to disseminate information amongst general public to spread awareness of Islamic banking.

Mahmood Ahmed (1998) tried to identify the attitude of 200 professional bankers and 200 bank customers in Bangladesh by using a purposive random sampling. It was found that both the groups have confusing thoughts about Islamic banking practices and thus given an argument that this misunderstanding has arise due to inadequate information of the basics of Sharia finance and because of the over-reliance on short term trade financing.

Metawa and Almossawi (1998) surveyed 300 customers of two commercial banks in Bahrain to investigate the banking behaviour of Islamic banking customers. They found the relationship of the customers' usage with their demographic factors, client's satisfaction with Sharia financial products and services, satisfaction with simple elements of services, they also found that customers chose religious factor to be the most important factor for bank selection criteria and convenience of the location was the least important factor.

Naser, Jamal and Al-Khatib (1999) in his study revealed that a large number of Sharia based bank clienteles in Jordan were pleased with Sharia banks' products and services and bank's repute and religion were the most substantial variables in bank selection criteria.

Erol and El-Bdour(1989) and Erol, Kaynak and El-Bdour(1990), had found that Jordanian Islamic bank clienteles were having understanding of Islamic ways of financing but less aware of financial services and products, because there were a small number of prospect customers of Islamic financing schemes.

Al-Sultan (1999) studied the perception of 385 customers in Kuwait for the Kuwait Finance House (KFH) an interest free bank. He confirmed that due to reasons of faith Kuwaitis are dealing with KFH, he also found out that there was no dissimilarities amongst cost and returns in KFH and another banks. Though, 51.7% of the respondents gave priority to deal with traditional banks as they provided improved service.

This implies even though Kuwaiti clients have religious justifications for using Sharia methods of financing and investment, they gave rankings to the quality services at the top of their bank selection criteria. These results are alike to those extracted by Haron, Ahmad and Planisek (1994) in Singapore.

Metwally (2002) conducted a research on the impact of demographic factors on clients' selection criteria in the state of Qatar where there is a dual banking system. The major findings were that females, older persons and public servants gave priority to transact with Sharia based Islamic banking institutions. There was another priority towards Sharia based Islamic banking establishments between peoples with low incomes and a semi illiterate. Conventional banks were mostly used by young male peoples in Qatar who were highly educated and professionals or good salaried government servants. Foreign banking institutions were also preferred by highly educated and high-income male clients.

Delta Khoirunissa (2003) used purposive sampling of 95 respondents to find out the motivating factors for customers' preference towards Islamic banking; it was found that the customers' decision is influenced by both economic factors such as monetary benefits, online facilities, religious factors, having good understanding on economic principles. The existence of the relationship between economic and religious preferences shows that in the choice of their banking criterion, the respondents wished to attain maximum satisfaction with regard to their economic and religious needs.

Okumus (2005) analyzed client gratification about interest free Sharia banking and bank selection criteria in Turkey, the research evaluated the magnitude of satisfaction and mindfulness of clienteles who were dealing with Special Finance Houses (SFH) that provided Islamic banking services. It was also observed that religion was perhaps the most important factor in motivating the clients for the use of Islamic banking products and services as found by previous studies by Omer(1992); Metwally; Metawa and Almossawi (2002) ; Al-Sultan and Bley and Kuehn(1999). The other motivating factor was the provision of traditional banking services by SFH. To summarize, there was a significant correlation among the extent of the client's satisfaction and factors for example age of the clienteles. Respondents in the 20-39 years age group were more satisfied with staff friendliness than other age groups.

Dusuki and Abdullah (2007) studied two Sharia banks' clienteles in Malaysia Bank Islamic Malaysia Berhad and Bank Muamalat Malaysia Berhad and examined the factors which motivate them in selection of Islamic banks. Their findings conferred with Erol and El-Bdour(1989), Erol, Kaynak and El-Bdour(1990), Haron, Ahmad and Planisek (1994)and Gerrard and Cunningham (1997), in which the quality of service delivery including staff friendliness and competency, efficient and speedy service were found to be important factors in influencing customers' banking selection.

MohdSaif Noman Khan, M. Kabir Hasan and Abdullah ibne Shahid (2007) also studied the banking behaviour of 100 customers of 5 Islamic banks in Dhaka and found that most of the customers of Islamic banks are highly educated and have a strong relationship with the banks.

Again religious motivation was the key reason for the choice of banks in this study as well.

Ahmad, W.M.W., et al., (2008) observed the role of religion in being the customers' choice of banking by using convenience sampling of 480 Muslims in Malaysia. Their findings reveal that there are major discrepancies in a Muslim's magnitude of adherence to religion and making Islamic bank as his choice for banking. They also suggested that Islamic banks should focus on developing electronic services and provide efficient and faster services to retain customers and attract more customers.

Gait and Worthington (n.d.) examined the perception, attitudes and motivation of 385 customers' Islamic banking customers in Libya through factors interpretations and discriminate analysis and revealed that respondent clients were aware of simple terms in Islamic banking like Qard Hassan and Musharka but unaware of terms like Mudarabah, bai muajjal and istisna. Four variables viz community service, profitability, religion, and unique services reflected the attitude of the respondents towards Islamic finance.

Mamunur Rashid and Kabir Hassan (2009) studied the effects of demographic variables on bank selection criteria of Sharia banks in Bangladesh by using regression analysis, controlled four factors such as gender, marital status, age and educational qualification. Their research revealed six variables such as corporal efficiency, core banking activities, compliance rules, convenience, confidence level and cost benefit analysis which help in determination of their choice for Sharia based Islamic banks.

AhsanulHaque, Jamil Osman and Ahmad ZakiHj Ismail (2009) studied the major variables influencing the client's awareness and contentment of Sharia based Islamic banks' clienteles in Malaysia and revealed that there exists a positive connection of quality of facilities confidence in bank, social and religious perspectives and availability of services with the customer perception about Islamic bank.

Sajeevan Rao and Sharma (2010) conducted a study to find out the bank selection criteria in 312 MBA students in Delhi and concluded that reliability is an important bank choice criterion.

Maran Marimuthu et al., (2010) did a study using non probability sampling among 450 respondents in Malaysia to find out the acceptance of Islamic banking and the factors responsible for it using chi square analysis. The results show that cost benefits, service delivery, convenience influence of friends/relatives were found to have significant relationship with the acceptance of Islamic banking for both Muslims and non-Muslims.

Muhammad Z Mamun (n.d.) studied 100 respondents from 11 Islamic banks and 13 such banks which offer dual i.e. both Islamic and conventional banking system in Bangladesh to study prospects and problems of Islamic banking and found that the adherence to the rules of Sharia make Islamic banking most attractive to the customers.

Idris, A.R. et al., (2011)studied the factors which play an important role in bank selection criteria by surveying 250Islamic bank customers in Malaysia found that religion is the main influencing factor. Other factors perceived to be important include ATM services, financial security, cost and benefit and attractiveness in that order.

Norafifah Ahmad and Sudin Haron (2000) in an exploratory research surveyed 45 corporate respondents from Kuala Lumpur for their perception of Islamic bank and found out that Islamic banking had a good potential as an alternative to conventional banking. Also they concluded that the most important factor for selection would be cost of services and products so Islamic banking has to maintain its cost low for services and products as compared to the conventional banking to retain and attract customers.

Hin C., et al. (2011) surveyed 270 students in one of the universities of Malaysia and examined the relationship between bank selection criteria and service quality towards the level of satisfaction and found that both bank selection criteria and service quality are main factors to determine the level of satisfaction towards a bank.

Asif, M. And Anjum, M., (2012)used multiple regression models to study the data collected from 45 Muslim customers of Peshawar KPK and found that a positive relationship exists between benefits of Islamic banking and its acceptance. The results of this study were similar to an earlier study by Dusuki and Abdullah (2007)

Hayat M. Awan and Khuram Shahzad Bukhari (2011) examined 250 respondents from four cities of Pakistan to know the bank selection criteria of customers of Islamic banks and found out that customers give more importance to the quality of services provided by Islamic banks and other features and not just the religion. Thus, they suggested focusing on quality of services and product features. Also they observed that the staffs were not able to provide credible information regarding religion.

Abdullah.M,, and Omar. M.A,(2012) interviewed 279 respondents to know about the Islamic bank selection criteria in Malaysia and found that religious attribute got the highest priority while profitability, banks' reputation, banks' status, facilities and services and friendly personnel were ranked in that order while an individual decides to support an Islamic bank.

Zarehan Selamat and Hazlina Abdul Kadir (2012) by using a random sampling technique on 150 customers in Malaysia found out that both Muslims and non-Muslim clients have an opinion in the bank selection and the religious motivation is not a major factor in the bank' selection process but provision of efficient facilities, privacy of the bank and banks' reputation and image were their main banking selection criterion.

Imtiaz Subhani et al., (2012) used a random sample of 300retail customers to find out the bank selection criteria in Pakistan and used t-test and found out that high returns and low service costs were one of the important influencing variables and religious sentiments and service quality were the secondary factors.

Sana Chebaband Houda Zribi (2012) surveyed 200 customers of Zaytuna bank in Tunisia who had moved from a conventional bank to an Islamic bank. The results showed that the most important factors which influenced their choice were quality of the relation customer/bank, diversity and quality of the banking services and the goodwill of the bank.

Nissar Ahmed Yatoo, S. Sudalai Muthu (2013) in a study in India revealed that Muslim people in India denote religious sentiments more than economic benefits about Islamic financial system. The result was based on studying the effect of demographic factors on the perception about the nature of Islamic methods of finance among 609 Indians.

Dineshwar Ramdhony (2013) examined the awareness and preference of investment in Islamic methods of finance among 232 Muslims and non Muslims in Mauritius and found that more than half of the respondents have heard of Islamic banking though the level of awareness was low. Respondents also suggested that religious beliefs and returns both motivate people to deal with Islamic banks. It was concluded that Muslims should not be the only focus of Islamic banks for prosperity.

H.Saduman Okumus and Elif GenerenGenc (2013) studied a random sample of 281 customers of bank in Turkey to know about their awareness and preference and found that most of the customers give importance to religious beliefs though it varied in demographic profile. Rate of returns was ranked last in the bank selection criteria. It was also found that there was a low level of satisfaction about the very limited number of branches and high service commission and fees.

Ramana Sheikh and Mohammad Faisal Ahammad (2013) obtained responses from both Muslims and non Muslims in the UK and found that there is a lack of awareness and understanding of the alternative banking system. Thus it was suggested that Islamic banks in UK should take aggressive measures of promotion and marketing of its products and services to spread awareness in the masses to increase potential customers.

Guyo, W and Adan, N. (2013) studied a random sample of 293 respondents in Kenya and found that the customers chose the bank without any religious motives though it was largely a Shariah compliant bank the range of financial options highly influenced the choice of the bank, good natured staff also scored high on the bank selection criteria, it can be concluded that religious beliefs scored lowest in bank selection criteria.

A study by Zeyad Saleem Ramadan (2013) in Jordan revealed that the bank selection criteria are a combination of both religious and other factors. The most important criteria were sociable personnel, Islamic reputation and image, and product price in the same order. It was concluded that Islamic banks cannot prosper just by attracting Muslims on their religious beliefs thus it is important to fulfil the needs of the customers and prospective customers to be in the market and face competition.

Zahidur Rahman, Md. Shariful Islam and Tahmina Akter (2013) did a survey of 52 customers of three branches of IBBL, Bangladesh to know about customer satisfaction and their bank selection criteria. The study revealed that customers irrespective of different demographic segments were mostly satisfied with IBBL and religious beliefs was the most important factor in bank selection criteria followed by bank's efficiency.

Nawi, F.A.M., Yazid, A.S and Mohammed, M.O (2013) in a study in Malaysia revealed that a new selection criteria of an Islamic bank should include understanding of the concept, Shariah compliance, quality and attraction of the products, prospects and potentials of Sharia based Islamic banking services and readiness to deal with Sharia banks.ss

Ranjbar A and Sharif S.P (n.d.) in an empirical study of 150 Muslims and Non Muslims respondents found that Muslims are more aware of the culture of Islamic banking and as a consequence more aware of the meaning of the fundamental terms used in Islamic banking and finance. There were differences between the Muslims and Non Muslims with regard to the attitudes towards Islamic banking. In regard to bank selection criteria, the factors which showed significant differences in Muslims and non Muslims were mass media advertising, credit on favourable terms, financial advice and location. There were no significant differences with regard to the other 18 factors. They concluded that Islamic banks need to offer fast and efficient services in order to attract more customers.

Kader et al.,(2014) in a study in Malaysia found using factor analysis that both Muslim and non Muslim customers are attracted to a bank due to its quality of service, its returns and repute, customers also look for other factors like service satisfaction, cost benefit when they are assured of religious factor.

It is also of utmost importance revealed from the literature that in the presence of large number of Sharia compliant banks available with people which bank they will opt for that depends not only on the choice of products available with the bank but also on improvement of customer service satisfaction, attractive cost benefit and provision of good bank ambience.

2.1.3 Studies Associated to Islamic Banking in India

Pandu, A., and Hussain, M.G., (2011) studied the introduction of Islamic banking in India and suggested a legal framework. They pointed out that though there are constraints in the implementation of Islamic banking in India due to the provisions in the Banking Regulations Act, special provisions could be created, on the lines of provisions for NBFCs, to permit Islamic banking in India to attract resources from the Middle Eastern countries which will result in better infrastructure facilities and this in turn will drive the economic growth of the country. They also suggested that initially, experimentation with existing models could be carried out and then RBI can issue licenses to global players in a phased manner to drive growth. Islamic windows could be opened in such ventures by following the examples set by secular countries like US, UK, France and Germany and then finally full-fledged Islamic banks can be made operational.

Ahangar G.B., Padder M.U.J and Ganie A.H. (2013) studied about Islamic banking and concluded that Islamic banking is not only fulfilling the needs of Muslim population but also develop other communities. As India is going to gain lot of benefits by attracting around US$ 1 trillion of Islamic funds for investment from Gulf countries this will aid the nation's economy and in fiscal deficit. It will not only help poor but also be fruitful for small manufacturers, retailers and agricultural enterprises to access finance and to provide equity finance for infrastructure facilities in India.

Jeet Singh and Preeti Yadav (2013) in a study of the growth and potential of Islamic banking stated that Islamic banking has been mistook in India as a religious charitable venture restricted only to the poverty-ridden and economically backward Muslim community. Even after years of successful Islamic banking operations and its phenomenal growth around the globe, it has failed to break this myth and therefore, RBI and the Ministry of Finance should also examine Islamic banking as a most viable alternative to tackle the macro-economic problems confronted in the country.

When Islamic banking will reach India, it should be seen as a progressive and modern alternative financial system and not as an undeveloped, aboriginal and obsolete finance method. It will be better for Indian economy and society to allow Islamic banks to operate and expand its network for the social well being and wealth generation activities in the society.

Khan K A (2013) in a study of need and scope of Islamic banking brought out that Islamic banking result in financial models that are not only profitable but also justly motivated. He concluded that the future prospects of Islamic banking in India is very good and it should be seen as "Interest free banking" through a broad spectrum and not through a narrow religious version.

Bhat, Z. A (2013) in a study observed that India needs huge capital for building its infrastructure, Islamic banking can provide interest-free loans to fulfil the need thus a lot of potential exists for Islamic banking in India. Though, at this stage it will need some solid policy decisions to make it happen. Also, it needs to be positioned as a professional banking entity rather than as a religion-based banking.

Basha, S.N. and Ahmed, M. (2013) studied the importance of Islamic banking in the Indian Economy and suggested that Indian government must seriously consider adopting Islamic banking as it would solve many economic problems faced by India like suicides of farmers, shutting down of small scale industries, increase in poverty and non inclusive growth. India may implement the same taking a cue from global examples like that of Singapore and UK.

Singh V.G., and Kaur, N. (2014) did a SWOT analysis for a view of Islamic banking concept and suggested a 10 point process to make it available for Indians. They suggested that it will be very challenging for Islamic banking to launch itself in India, and Islamic banking products should not be rigid in its practices and should offer variety of products and services meant for the people of India and also it should not be confined to any particular community and should be available for all.

A recent study by Aisha Badruddin (2015) made suggestions based on the fact that there is a non availability of any reports on the economic feasibility of Islamic banking and its impact on the inclusive growth in India. Also suggested there should be proper training and education be given in this area by including Islamic banking in curriculum of professional courses. As Islamic banking cannot be adopted in the present legal framework in India thus India needs to follow the lines of the UK and introduce new laws to govern Islamic banking in India.

The current state of literature suggests that Islamic Banking has played an important role in a country's economic growth. In the thought process over allowing Islamic banking in the country, experts have pointed out that it is a question of "how soon and not whether it will be allowed", as it can help a fund-starved country to get long-term finances. "It is not when, but how soon, the Reserve Bank and the government will take a positive view on this highly effective financing option," T Balakrishnan, who was behind the formation of Al Barakah Financial Services, promoted by the Kerala government, mentioned in a meet on Islamic banking organised by the Indo-Arab chamber of Commerce and Industries. (Financial Express, 27, November, 2011)

2.1.4 Studies in Support of Islamic Banking

There are abundant arguments in support of Islamic scholars in the Western literature as the Western economists have found links in interest rates and instability in macro economy which affects almost all the capitalist economies like unemployment, negative growth and inflation. (Mill 1826, Smith 1904, Keynes 1931, Fisher 1933, Hayek 1933, 1939, Wicksell 1935, Minsky 1977, Greenwald and Stiglitz 1988, Bernante and Gertler 1990)

This western literature support interest free banking and should strengthen the Islamic scholar's arguments about interest free banking and they should take an empirical approach. Though western economics is based on classical economics which has a basis of a perfect world but they have made progress with the acceptance of uncertainty and imperfections and test economic theories empirically. While the Islamic theory describes "how people, groups or governments should act in a perfect Islamic community" and people do not act as expected thus empirical tests have to be done to know Muslims' behaviour in the real world towards Islamic Banking.

Friedman (1969) made suggestions that a zero interest rate is a basic condition for most advantageous distribution of resources. It was also found that a zero rate of interest is sufficient for efficient allocation within general equilibrium models (Wilson, 1979; Cole and Kocherlakota, 1998). Literature is also in support that interest-free or profit and loss sharing system is feasible and better to an interest-based system (Chapra, 1985, Mirakhor, 1997).

Waseem Ahmad (2008) found out Islamic banking system started in 2003 in United Kingdom given to its popularity and reception in less than five years it stands out as a prominent financial player in the UK financial market and Islamic banking has greater opportunities to grow in the UK due to its Muslim community from South Asia which mostly come from Pakistan, India and Bangladesh because these people are financially sound and play their role as an active member of UK economy.

Basainey Ebrahima Jammeh (2010) stated that though there is a decline in consumer confidence in the US financial institutions due to the financial crisis, the future for Islamic financial institutions seems promising due to the strong performance shown by Islamic house mortgages during the recent financial crisis. This is the major reason why Islamic banking has become a buzzword.

Mubashshir Asrar (2011) has found that Islamic banking is just not confined to just lending interest free loans but it is a package of Sharia compliant services which has a good potential market in India. In a study by Grail research it was found that if there are favourable regulatory conditions, India holds a promising position for opportunity for Islamic financial institutions whose assets are to going to be more than triple to what is approximately $ 1 trillion.

As Siddiqi (2002) shared that research in Islamic economics has showed that without interest also economic system can function smoothly. With a system in which profit sharing models, trade based modes that are Murabahah and leasing, etc is used will prove to be more efficient, stable and equitable as compared to the interest based system.

It is rightly pointed out by Siddiqi (2007) that a trend of decline in bonds and a rise in equity for a means of investment can be seen both at international and domestic levels. People are making ethical considerations while making their choice for growth of wealth. This opens a window for Islamic finance to serve balanced growth, mutuality and equitable distribution and humanity.

Modern researchers have concluded that interest has led to dire consequences in the economy. It has resulted in inappropriate allocation of resources which leads to instability in the system. This further has led to increase in inequality in the distribution of wealth and income and which results in rich becoming richer and poor becoming poorer.

Siddiqi (2009) suggested that once interest is taken out from the economy then speculation can also be in reasonable limits. There should be transparency whenever it is the matter of people's money and the society should insist on transparency. Dissemination of information should be smooth which can help minimize uncertainty. Gambling on stock market can be in check or betting on risks would be easier to eliminate. Other people's interest should be given a priority and mutuality should be considered while taking financial decisions.

"In the Persian Gulf region and Asia, Standard & Poor's estimates that 20 per cent of banking customers would now spontaneously choose an Islamic financial product over a conventional one with a similar risk-return profile. The Vatican has put forward the idea that the principles of Islamic finance may represent a possible cure for ailing markets."Lorenzo Totaro (2009)

In another study it was found that it was projected that in 2008 the beginning of financial crisis could have been avoided if the world's financial institutions had followed Sharia. As Islamic finance is mostly concentrated in property assets and is subject to market fluctuations of those assets only. Charles A. Rarick(2010)

Most of the findings of the studies are concurrent with the previous literature on the effectiveness of Interest free banking as a banking practice, except for the profitability and asset quality ratios. Due to the reason as Islamic banks earn lower net income than conventional banks. Another reason could be that Islamic banks book higher impaired loans than the conventional banks in comparison to conventional bank's gross loans. This needs further research in knowing credit and provisioning policies for both the banks. (Ahmed, pandey, 2010)

Ahmad Khalil, (2012) puts forth an argument which suggests that Indian Muslims have customised the commercial banks services and satisfied with the current banking system. As the author interviewed bank executives of the personal banking division and found out that a significant Muslim population do not invest in mutual funds which have a debt component, and they donate the interest from their savings account for charity or they prefer current account than the savings account.

In a similar study by Mohamed Hisham Yahya, Junaina Muhammad, Abdul Razak Abdul Hadi, (2012) revealed that though Shariah Compliant banks are bound by tenets of Islam in operations but still their performance is at par with conventional banks.

Keeping in mind the recommendations of the Raghuram Rajan Committee The RBI had got references from the Indian Centre for Islamic Finance to introduce interest free banking in India for ensuring inclusive growth for all and innovation in the banking techniques to suit their needs. (Financial Express 27 March 2012).

"Finally, it would also be necessary to deregulate interest rates in order to unlock funds to activities that are commercially unviable and therefore denied credit. Current priority sector norms especially those focused on lending to the poor (loans below Rs 2 lakhs) have interest rate ceilings that make lending unattractive for the banks. In general, the true cost of small loans is very high. This is also reflecting by the interest rates currently paid by the poorest borrowers, which is typically in the range of 36 per cent plus per annum". Report of the Committee on Financial Sectors Reforms, Planning Commission of India (2009)

It is also important to mention that the component of micro financing has been missing from Islamic Banking as pointed out by Abdul Rahim Abdul Rahman (2007) "that Islamic finance has an important role for furthering socio-economic development of the poor and small (micro) entrepreneurs without charging interest or riba. Furthermore, Islamic financing schemes have moral and ethical attributes that can effectively motivate micro entrepreneurs to thrive and proposed to accommodate the Islamic microfinance within the present Islamic banking structure."

Another study by Khan Ajaz Khurram (2013) suggests that Islamic banking in India has a lot of scope in India as it will contribute significantly in the country's economic growth, boost entrepreneurship skills in India, will be able to make a provision of low cost capital to small entrepreneurs also to needy consumers and thus would compliment conventional banking system.

The scope and potential of Islamic Banking has also been highlighted by Bhat Ahmad Zameer (2013) that the RBI has made efforts to give relaxation in interest rates so that liquidity can be enhanced as the country is largely dependent on funds from West, which is not stable in these years and this leads to depreciation in the value of rupee and thus to inflation and thus the economy is trapped in this vicious circle. Thus it is all the more important to take notice and try to implement Sharia principles which have proven to be more stable in such times.

A study in the UK by Ahmad (2008) shows that to cater the needs of Muslim population Sharia Banking came in UK and the findings from the research shows that there is a good potential for growth of Sharia based financial system as the Muslim population is ready to accept financial products which are interest free and are willing to spend their living as per their faith. Though as the financial products and awareness is concerned the community needs to be educated and information dissemination by the banks has to be improved as to survive with the conventional banking system in the banking sector with the given regulations and supervisions.

Zehri and Al-Herch (2013) concluded that "the Islamic Banks are less affected by the recent crisis. It does not mean that Islamic Banks are not at all affected by the financial crisis, however it explain, as pointed out by different calls of experts and economists that the Islamic Banks are less susceptible to the financial crisis . In fact, the very nature of the Islamic banking, the prohibition of dealing in derivative and speculative assets has served to protect Islamic banks from the adverse effects of the economic crisis."

Islamic Banking has also proven to be effective in wealth creation as suggested by Ismail (2010) "The role of Islamic banks includes: to clear and settle payments; to aggregate (pool) and disaggregate wealth and allow the flow of funds so that both large-scale and small-scale projects can be financed; to transfer economic resources over time, locations and sectors; to accumulate, process and disseminate information for decision-making purposes; to provide ways for managing uncertainty and controlling risk; and to provide ways for dealing with risk and return issues that arise in financial contracting. These roles can be performed by offering financial transactions, pooling savings and channelling funds. By performing these roles, Islamic banks play a valuable and integral part in the development of the national economy by creating wealth for individuals and the community."

One of the studies to relate economic growth with Islamic Banking done by Johnson Katherine(2013) show that "the effect of Islamic banking on financial deepening is dependent on the legal origin of the countries in which it operates. Islamic banks are negatively correlated with financial system development in countries of British legal origin and positively correlated in countries with French legal origin. This outcome indicates that Islamic banks may be more beneficial to development of the financial sector in French legal origin countries. Muslim populations are underserved financially and predominantly come from less developed countries, rendering Islamic banking a potential tool for growth. Even though a fairly new institution, Islamic banks are growing at a rapid rate and affecting the societies in which they take root. Consequently, their impact may become more apparent as the sector continues to grow."

An empirical study of analysis of attitudes, perceptions and knowledge of conventional financial institution products and services by Worthington (2007) suggests that "in terms of individual consumers, the evidence to date suggests that the presence of Islamic finance involves a substantial degree of market segmentation. While religious conviction is a logical key determinant of the use of Islamic finance services, it is often not the only concern, with most consumers also identifying bank reputation, service quality and pricing as being of relevance in determining their patronage of a particular financial institution. That said, at least some studies have found little evidence of substantial differences in the key features of Islamic and conventional finance products and services, suggesting that religious conviction may have a role to play at the margin. But problematically for the Islamic finance industry, the level of knowledge of Islamic finance methods is generally low among individual consumers, especially among immigrant communities and countries with an Islamic finance system yet to be established. This place a heavy emphasis on the development of marketing and information programs to coincide with the introduction of new institutions, products and services."

2.2 Research Methodology

The research methodology adopted to conduct the present study has been discussed in the following paragraphs:

2.2.1 Research Framework

To answer the research questions the variables needed to be identified into dependent and independent variables. The prospects of Islamic banking in India is dependent on certain factors like awareness of the people, attitude, motivating factors, implementation and thus prospect is a dependent variable and the factors mentioned above are independent variables.

2.2.2 Research Questions

This kind of analysis has been taken up in conventional banking system but in Islamic banking system very few studies have been done. Mir (2014) showed retail banking consumers, enterprises, employees in Jammu and Kashmir State for identifying the factors responsible for forming attitudes for establishment of Islamic Banking in India. In the present study the consumer banking clients are taken as sample to find out their attitudes, awareness towards Islamic Banking in India. Also motivating factors given by Mir (2014) has been taken to find out whether these factors will motivate consumer banking clients to go for Islamic banking or not. Also it is important to know how people are using the present banking system to make it interest free and what problems they are facing to do so. Finally it is important to know if Islamic Banking comes into existence what changes are going to take place in their opinion.

So to answer the question of Prospects of Islamic banking in India some more questions need to be answered like:

1. Do people have any understanding about the Sharia Banking in India?
2. What is the perception of clients towards Islamic Banking in India?
3. What are the motivating factors for potential use of Islamic Banking in India?
4. Are people applying any methods of Islamic finance?
5. Is there any impact of education on preference of Islamic banking methods?

2.2.3 Research Approach

A rational research approach is required for the validity of any social research. In order to test the awareness, preferences, willingness, perception, opinion of people towards Sharia banking system a survey was conducted on respondents in NCT of Delhi.

Research design

For this purpose convenience sampling was used for 311 respondents in NCT of Delhi. The pilot study was done for 60 respondents to judge the reliability of the questionnaire. The results of the pilot study have been discussed in chapter 6.

Questionnaire construction

On the basis of instruments designed by Mir,2014, Yusuf,1999 & Loo, 2010, Gerrard and Cunningham, 1997, Ahmad & Haron,2002, Ansari Rehan, 2009 a questionnaire given in Appendix-1 consisting 52 questions measuring the variables of the study was developed as an instrument for survey. For factor analysis questions on demographic profile were also included. In order to test the reliability of the questionnaire it was tested on 60 representative respondents during the pilot study.

The questionnaire was divided into four sections as per the factors identified for the research which are Awareness denoted by AW, Motivational factors denoted by MF, Attitude denoted by AT, Implementation denoted by IM and Application denoted by AP. For measuring awareness amongst the various users of commercial banking it was asked to them about presence of Islamic banking and its various functions using the same term as in Islamic banking for better understanding of the terms, it was explained in simple English as the terms were in Arabic. This section was styled on those used by Mir (2014) and Cunningham (2009). Mir (2014) did this study in Jammu & Kashmir state only focusing on to the stakeholders of Islamic banking majorly comprising of businessmen who might be interested in financing by Islamic banks while the current study in the state of Delhi and NCR comprising of the people who are commercial bank clients. Cunningham (2009) conducted the study in Singapore where at that time, did not have Islamic Banking. The second section is of motivational factors which could be responsible for investment in Islamic banking which is styled in the same way as used by Mir (2014). The next section comprises of questions related measurement of attitude, and in the next section questions are related to the application part of Interest free financial transactions practiced by the respondents, and finally the last section deals with questions related to the implementation of Islamic banking system in India.

2.2.4 Data Collection Method

Based on previous researches the factors responsible for the success of Sharia based Islamic banking system were identified and thus were used in taking the survey through primary sources by distributing the questionnaire online and offline.

Published data from national journal and international journal was also used for the study after testing its reliability.

2.2.5 Sample Size

Sample size was taken as 311 consisting of 157 Muslims and 154 Non Muslims amongst the parts of Delhi & NCR.

2.2.6 Sampling Design

To carry out the present study convenience sampling method was used for drawing the sample out of the defined population. The sample consisting of 311 people was used amongst which people had different occupations businessmen, students, private and public servants. All of them were having their accounts in conventional banking system. They were administered questionnaire through survey method.

Now, it is necessary to give a view of Indian banking structure on Indian land existing in diversified religious and cultural views where to find out possibility of interest free banking culture as per Sharia financial system in Islam. Hence, the next chapter is devoted to banking system in India.

CHAPTER-3

BANKING SYSTEM IN INDIA: A SYNOPTIC VIEW

The present chapter is devoted to present the banking scenario in India from legal and operative angles to examine the possibilities of introducing and running successfully the zero interest banking system given in Sharia financial system in Islam.

3.1 Introduction

The Indian financial system is divided into two constituents, first is comprised of organized banking and financial institutions and the second comprised of unorganized persons and institutions. The Reserve Bank of India is the central bank which controls all commercial banks, development banks, cooperative banks and other organized banking institutions coming under the definition of bank. The Banking system in India is comprised of the Reserve Bank of India, the State Bank of India, commercial banks, exchange banks, the industrial banks, the indigenous bankers, the co-operative banks and the land development banks. Before its establishment, the three presidency banks, in Calcutta, Bombay and Madras during the first half of the 19th century were functioning. These banks had a monopoly of banking business and a partial monopoly of note issue. They had been allowed to use government balances free of charge in the presidency towns. But they had restrictions in dealing with foreign bills and thus could not borrow money from abroad. They could make advances till six months and could issue loans only on movable property. Several proposals were made to amalgamate these banks but were rejected. It was only in 1920 the Imperial Bank of India came into existence by merging these Presidency Banks.

3.2 Evolution and Development of Banking System in India

Banking during the pre British period was generally carried on by the indigenous bankers. Towards the end of the 18th century, the East India Company setup some Agency houses to carry on the important banking activities. In 1921, Imperial Bank of India was established which later on became State Bank of India. The need to establish a central bank was being realised which resulted in the establishment of the Reserve Bank of India.

Pre Independence Era

The Banking Ordinance of 1946 helped Reserve Bank of India to maintain a close watch over the banking system in India as RBI, lender of last resort as bankers' bank. The reason why most of the banks failed in that period was that they were largely exposed to speculative ventures. The loss of depositor's money had eventually led to the loss of their interest in banking with the banks.

3.2.1 Reserve Bank of India (RBI)

The Reserve Bank of India, is the main regulatory bank in India to control all the banking and financial institutions in India. It was established in 1935 by legislation of the Government of India. It has the authority to perform the following activities under Reserve Bank of India Act:

i) Currency issuing authority- it is the sole authority of RBI to issue currency notes in the economy. All the notes issued by RBI have legal identity everywhere in India. Besides this, RBI has also been empowered with the authority to circulate and withdraw the currency from circulation.

ii) Monitoring Authority- the RBI is known as the Banker's Bank because it has all the authority to banking system in India. The RBI controls the deposits of the commercial banks through CRR, SLR. Since commercial banks can borrow money from the Reserve bank of India when they are in need of finance. Therefore, RBI is the lender of last resort.

iii) Banker to Union Government- RBI provides wide range of banking services to the both Union government and state government. It also transfers the funds, collects receipts, and makes the payment on behalf of the government. Public debts are also managed by the RBI. Thus, it deals in treasury bills.

iv) Foreign Exchange Regulation Authority- another main function of RBI is to control the foreign exchange reserves position. RBI has been empowered with the authority to prescribe the exchange rate system, to maintain a better relation between rupee and other currencies, to interact with the foreign counterparts and to manage the foreign exchange reserves. It deals and controls foreign exchange reserves.

3.2.2 SBI Act, 1955

In order to strengthen the functioning of RBI, the need was to establish a large commercial bank under the control of the Government to implement the monetary policy of RBI in letter and spirit, SBI came into existence in 1955 by converting the Imperial Bank of India by State Bank of India Act. At present, it is the largest Government commercial bank of India with regard to deposit mobilization and branch expansion. It has been compelled by RBI to spread over its functioning in urban, semi-urban and also in rural areas. This bank is modern banker on interest based system.

3.2.3 The Banking Regulation Act, 1949

The Banking Regulation Act, 1949 specifies provisions relating to registration and governance of commercial pattern banks.

In case of foreign banks, 20% of the profits from operations are required to be deposited with the RBI, in India every year. However, an exemption is given in certain cases.

Preamble

This Act applies to following categories of banks:

1. Nationalised Banks
2. Non- nationalised Banks
3. Co-operative Banks.

Following are some of the significant provisions prescribed with the objective of controlling and regulating the Indian Banking.

- The requirements for the minimum owned capital and reserves for commencement of banking business, prohibition of interest charges on calls in arrears or unpaid amount of capital and payment of Dividends only after writing off all Capitalized expenses.
- Minimum 20 per cent of profits must be transferred to statutory liquidity reserve funds and 3 percent needs to be kept as cash reserves. Banking companies are restricted from holding shares in other companies.
- There are restrictions for granting loans and advances to directors etc. Licenses are necessary for setting up new branches and transfer of existing business to other institutions.
- A banking institution is directed through this Act to maintain Assets (Minimum 75 per cent of DTL) in India and submit the Return of unclaimed Deposits with the prescribed authority.

1. This Act prescribes banking companies to prepare books of Accounts, final statements and get them audited as well as publish the relevant information

about financial performance and position of the company. The RBI is authorised to inspect books of Accounts of banking companies.

2. It is necessary for a banking company to get prior approval from RBI for appointment as well as termination of managing directors, and other managerial personnel, employees etc.

3. Under this Act the RBI is authorised to appoint additional directors in a banking company.

4. Suspension under the orders of a High Court.

5. Winding up of banking companies.

6. The Central Government is authorised for granting orders of mortal rim as well as for reconstruction and amalgamation banking enterprises.

7. The RBI is powered to examine the financial records and may tender advice for closing the banking institution.

8. The RBI is authorised to inspect a banking company and make report about its winding up.

9. The RBI is also powered to call for Returns and other relevant information from the Liquidator of a Banking company.

10. The RBI Issues No Objection Certificate to banking companies in case banks want to make changes in the name of a banking company.

11. The RBI also issues No objection certificate for the Alteration and changes in the memorandum of a banking company. Central Government is statutorily obliged to consult the RBI for making rules regarding banking companies. The monetary authority of India viz., RBI also recommends the Central Government for exempting any bank from the provisions of this Act.

Capital and Reserves Requirements

The requirements for authorized and owned capital and also the reserves have been mentioned under section 11 of this Act which prescribes capital adequacy from time to time for Indian banks. While on the other hand foreign banks which intends to set up banking business in India are required to have a minimum of ten million US dollars to India in the form of Capital. The minimum capital required to start a Local Area Bank prescribed by RBI is Rs. 500 crores.

According to the provisions given under Section 12, the company's subscribed capital may be half of its authorized capital.

Section 14 Provisions

Under Section 14, all banking companies have been prohibited from levying any charge upon its unpaid capital, and any such charges or levy, if created, shall be invalid.

Limiting the payment of dividends: Section 15

Under the provisions of Section 15, all banking companies have been prohibited from paying any dividend on its shares unless it has completely written off all capitalized expenses specified in the balance sheet of the companies.

As per this section, no banking institution shall provide any dividends on shareholdings unless and until all of its capitalized expenses e.g. preliminary expenses, brokerage and commission on the issue of shares must be completely written off.

However as per the Banking Companies (Amendment) Act 1956, Banking Institution may pay dividend on shareholdings without writing off the specified expenditures.

Transfer to Reserve Fund: Section 17

Section 17 requires banking companies incorporated under the Banking Regulation Act-1949 in India, to transfer an amount, not less than 20% of the profit every year except in specified situation.

Maintenance of cash reserves by non-scheduled banks: Section 18

Non-Scheduled Banks need to maintain cash reserve with itself or with Reserve Bank of India or specified bank, at least 3% of its total time and demand deposits.

Restrictions on holding of shares in other companies: Section 19

Section 19 of the Act limits the scope of formation of subsidiary companies by a banking institution, as well as the holding of shares in other companies. That is, this section restricts banking companies getting involved trading activities by acquiring a controlling interest in non-banking companies. We may conclude that this section restricts the scope of formation of subsidiary companies by a banking company, as well as the holding of shares in other companies. The subsidiary banks can be formed subject to the previous permission in writing of the RBI.

Restrictions on loans and advances: Sections 20 & 21

Section 20 lays down the restrictions on banking companies from granting any loan to any of its directors or to any firm in which a director is interested or to any individual or whom a director stands as a guarantor. Further the banking companies are prohibited from granting loans or advances on the security of its own shares.

RBI gives directions to banking companies on the matters relating to advances, margin money, and rate of interest, maximum amount of loan, reserves and also the deposits of the concerned bank.

Licensing system for banking companies: Section 22

According to this section, no banking company can commence or carry on any business of banking in India unless it holds a licence granted to it by the Reserve Bank of India for the said purpose. This section states the following requirements for granting licence:

(i) Necessity of licensing and mode of applying for it.

(ii) Conditions for granting of licenses.

(iii) Cancellation of licenses and appeals of existing banking companies.

Thus, every banking company which intends to start banking business in India must obtain licence from RBI, the monetary authority of India.

Control on the opening of new business: Section 23

The RBI under this section has to supervise and regulate the starting of new banking businesses and its transfer.

Maintenance of statutory liquid assets or reserve (SLR): Section 24

Under this section, every banking company in India shall maintain a certain proportion of liquid assets as per directives of RBI from time to time. The liquid assets include cash, gold or unencumbered approved securities.

Maintenance of Assets in India: Section 25

Section 25 requires for the maintenance of assets equivalent to at least 75% of its demand and time deposits or liabilities in India, at the close of business of the last Friday of every quarter.

Submission of Returns of unclaimed Deposits: Section 26

As per this section, every banking company shall submit a return of operated accounts in India. Various other returns as per requirements are also to be submitted to RBI under section 27. Under section 28, RBI is authorized to publish any information obtained as per Banking Regulation Act in public interest. Annual financial statements are also to be prepared in respect of banking business in India and outside India. Annual financial statements are to be audited by statutory auditor as per requirements.

Apart from the Banking Regulation Act for governing commercial banks in public, private and co-operative sectors, the legal framework of financial institutions for large, medium and small industries has been provided by Union Government and also by State Governments. This framework led to the development of industrial banks namely Industrial Development Bank of India (IDBI), Industrial Finance Corporation of India (IFCI), State Financial Corporations and so on. In the succeeding paragraphs few representative banks' legal framework is discussed. Thus, the financial system in India comprises of: the Reserve Bank of India, the commercial banks i.e. public, private and foreign banks, the exchange banks i.e. export import bank, the co-operative banks, the agricultural banks i.e. NABARD, LDBs, the non banking financial institutions such as IDBI, ICICI, UTI, SFC, LIC, GIC etc. and the registered and unregistered mutual funds. Some important legislations for development banks and financial corporations have also been enacted by appropriate Governments.

3.2.4 Banking Developments in Post Independence Era

With Independence a lot of changes had taken place in India. In 1947, over 600 commercial banks were there in the country. But large firms were given preference in terms of lending credit whereas small scale enterprises have to face huge difficulty in case they needed credit. This led to nationalization of Imperial Bank and form State Bank of India in 1955. This paved the way of social control on banking institutions.

(i) Social Control over Banking

In 1969, 14 major commercial banks were nationalized and 6 more banks were further nationalized in 1980. The Two main purposes of nationalization were providing credit according to the planned priorities and rapid branch expansion. Thus, in order to achieve regional balance banking facilities were extended to uncovered areas. Nationalization resulted branch expansion in urban, semi-urban and rural areas and growth in deposit mobilization.

By the end of 1980s, the Indian banking sector was facing several structural problems like financial unsoundness, unprofitability and inefficiency. Going by the international standards, the Indian banks were extremely unprofitable despite having a rapid growth of deposits, although impressive progress was made by the banks in the two decades following nationalization, the excessive controls enforced on them by the government resulted in the rigidities and inefficiencies in the commercial banking system. This not only combated their development but also eroded their profitability.

(ii) Post Liberalization financial and banking sector Reforms:-

The year 1991 was a changing point in India's economic policy. Balance of payments crisis in 1991 has initiated the structural reforms. Mixed economy approach was followed and the private sector became more prominent.

The Narsimham Committee

The need was felt to rectify the deficiencies of Indian financial sector towards economic liberalization. Hence, under the chairmanship of Shri. M. Narasimhama high level committee was constituted to review the progress and working of the Indian financial sector and to suggest some measures to reform it. The following are the rigidities and weakness in the system found out by the committee:

The Narasimham committee pointed out that the reason for the poor profitability of Indian banks were pre-emption of funds by government in the form of statutory liquidity requirements, overstaffing, its priority sector lending, lack of organization and a proper work culture and excessive controls on opening and closing of branches, including the policy of fostering unviable bank branches. Therefore reforms were recommended by the committee to revamp the banking system so as to make it competitive and efficient.

Narsimham Commitee Recommendations

The Government of India formed a committee under the chairmanship of Mr. Narsimham, former Governor, Reserve Bank of India to examine the structure and functioning of the existing financial system of India and suggest suitable reforms. The committee submitted its report in 1991. The recommendations made by the Committee are as follows:

1. Banks need to restore their structure so as to have three to four large banks.
2. Local bank should operate only in specified regions.
3. Atleast 8-10 national banks with a network of branches throughout the country should be engaged in 'Universal' banking. Rural banks should be confined to rural areas mainly to finance agriculture and allied activities and should also focus on profitability.
4. Rural banking subsidiaries should be set up by each public sector bank to take over all its rural branches.
5. RRBs should undertake all types of banking business
6. The practice of branch licensing should be abolished and individual banks should have the freedom to open or close any branch.

7. Foreign banks should have the same requirements as Indian banks were having.
8. Foreign operations of the Indian banks should be rationalised.
9. Computerisation of bank operations should be done.
10. Freedom should be given to Individual banks to recruit their officers.
11. Inspection by supervisory staff should be guided by internal audit.
12. The Reserve Bank of India should be the primary agency for regulating the banking system.
13. A separate authority under The Reserve bank of India should be set up to regularise banks and other financial institutions.
14. There should not be any involvement of politics in appointment of Chief Executives and Directors of the banks.
15. Cash Reserve ratio should be progressively reduced.
16. Statutory Liquidity ratio should be brought down to 25% over the next five years.
17. The priority sector should be redefined.
18. Direct Credit programmes should be phased out.
19. Interest rate should be deregulated so as to reflect emerging market trends.
20. Uniform accounting practices should be adopted by the banks.
21. Balance sheet of the banks should be transparent.
22. The commercial banks should achieve a minimum 4% capital adequacy ratio in relation to risk weighted assets by March 1993.
23. Government should constitute special tribunals for the quick recovery of loans.

24. ARF or an Assets Reconstruction Fund should be formed to take over from banks and financial institutions a portion of their non performing assets at a discount.

Measures taken to improve the Banking system

1. Capital Adequacy Norms: All the banks were required to achieve a risk weighted capital adequacy ratio of 4% by 31 March1993 and 8% by 31 March 1996. Foreign banks in India and Indian banks operating abroad had to achieve 8% norm by 31 March 1993 and 31 March 1994 respectively.
2. Prudential Accounting Norms: if interest or instalment of principal is in arrears for any two quarters in the accounting year the credit facility will be treated as non performing asset.
3. Recapitalisation: With a view to enable the public sector banks to meet the capital adequacy ratio the government of India contributes to the capital of such banks.
4. Recovery of Bad Debts: The Recovery of Bad Debt due to banks and Financial Institutions Act, 1993 had been passed to constitute debt recovery tribunals.
5. Partial Privatisation of Public sector banks: In view of the limited resources of the government, banks had been allowed to mobilise equity resources from the public. For this purpose the State bank of India Act was amended and the Reserve bank of India share holding had been reduced to 67%.
6. Freedom to open Branches: Banks were allowed to open new branches and extend counters after attainment of the prescribed capital adequacy norms.

7. Entry of Private sector banks: To provide better customer services and promote competition private banks were allowed to be set up as per RBI guidelines.
8. Department of Supervision: A department of supervision was set up in RBI from 22 December 1993 to supervise the working of commercial banks.
9. Banking Ombudsman Scheme: The scheme started from June 1995 for quick and economical settlement of customer complaints about the deficiencies in banking services.
10. Board for Financial Supervision: The Board was set up in the RBI in 1994 for implementation of regulations in the field of income recognition, credit management, asset classification, provisioning and capital adequacy, etc.
11. Scheme of Disclosure regarding Defaulting borrowers: The scheme of disclosure of defaulting borrowers with outstanding aggregating to Rs. 1 crore and above as on 31 March and 30 September every year was introduced in April, 1994.
12. Central Board of Bank frauds: The Finance Ministry, Government of India had set up a Board in January 1997 for rendering advice on cases being pursued by the CBI against bank officials up to the level of Manager.
13. Consortium Arrangement: Large borrowers above a specified credit limit have been allowed to operate through consortium of scheduled commercial banks headed by a lead bank.
14. Liberalisation of lending norms: The banks can now decide the levels of holding of individual items of inventory and receivables to be permitted to

borrowers and also the quantum and period of ad hoc credit limits without charging additional interest.

15. Measures to streamline working of banks: Measures like management information systems and the internal audit and control mechanisms, computerisation of banking operations; prudential norms for income recognition assets, etc have been introduced to improve the quality of performance and management of banks.

16. Liberal Credit Control Measures: SLR on incremental net demand and time liabilities has been reduced to 25%.

17. New Private Banks: For allowing greater participation by private sector banks, the RBI issued in guidelines in 2001 as:

    (a) The banks should have a minimum paid up capital of Rs. 200 crore to be raised to Rs.300 crore within three years of the start of a business.

    (b) The promoters' stake should be 40%.

    (c) NRI contribution in primary equity not to exceed 40%.

    (d) The new bank cannot be promoted by any large business house, but individual companies can contribute upto 10% equity.

    (e) NBFCs with AAA rating and 12% capital adequacy can function as a bank.

    (f) The new bank will have to maintain a capital adequacy ratio of 10%.

    (g) The total net bank credit 40% will be for priority sector lending.

    (h) 25% of the branches of the new bank should be in rural or semi urban areas.

18. Entry into Insurance Business: Any bank fulfilling the above criteria, and with a minimum net worth of Rs.500 crore, can undertake insurance business.

The Government of India constituted another Committee under the chairmanship of Mr. Narsimham specifically to suggest measures for reforming the banking sector. The Committee submitted its report in April 1998. The report covered a wide range of issues like capital adequacy, bank management, bank legislation, bank mergers, etc. The main recommendations are as follows:

(a) Stronger Banking System: The Committee laid great emphasis on the need of a stronger banking system particularly in the context of capital account convertibility which will necessarily involve huge flows of capital to and from the country, and would require cautious management of exchange rate and domestic liquidity. Thus Committee recommended merger of stronger banks. The Committee had cautioned on merger of weak and stronger banks as this may dilute the asset quality of the stronger bank.

(b) Narrow Banking: For the rehabilitation of weak banks with high NPAs the Committee had suggested the concept of narrow banking that is these banks should lodge their funds in short term risk free assets.

(c) Small Local Banks: The Committee suggested the establishment of small local banks to serve the needs of a state or even a cluster of districts in respect of agriculture, small industry and trade.

(d) Capital Adequacy: To improve the strength and risk absorption capacity of banks the Committee suggested raising their capital adequacy ratio. It was also suggested for the establishment of an Asset Reconstruction Fund (ARF) to take over the NPAs of the banks.

(e) Real Autonomy: The Committee has strongly pleaded for withdrawing ownership of government and control of banks and providing greater independence and flexibility in the functioning of public sector banks. The RBI should perform only regulatory functions and not intervene in management of the banks on a day to day basis.

(f) Review of Banking Laws: The committee has stressed on an urgent review of all the banking laws and amendment of their provisions to fulfil the current requirements of the banking industry.

With all these recommendations being put into practice we have a banking system which can be seen in present times in which lot of technological advances have been made and a host of financial services are taking place. Below are some of the new services provided in the current banking system:

1. Electronic Fund Transfer (EFT): EFT is quick and simple transfer of funds from one place to another. With it a person can send money on the same day or next day.

2. Credit Card: With the help of a credit card a customer can purchase goods and services from merchants who have the swipe machine (EDC) without making immediate cash payments but, within the prescribed limit given by the bank.

3. Debit Card: With a Debit Card a person can make payments or purchases and the amount is deducted from one's account. The debit card also needs to be swiped on the EDC or swipe machine and the PIN has to be entered by the debit card holder.

4. Phone banking: The Phone banking officer can help with all the information related to bank account and provide services like, loans, credit cards, etc. subject to approval by the bank.
5. Telebanking: Telebanking or IVR (Interactive Voice Response) is a banking facility which based on the voice processing facility available on bank computers available. In this case, banking services or products are provided to its clients through telephone.
6. Internet Banking: Internet Banking provides a host of financial services like open accounts, pay bills, know account balances, view and print copies of cheques, stop payments, funds transfer, etc.
7. Mobile Banking: as the name suggest, banking with the help of mobile is knows as mobile banking. Anyone having a mobile phone can have an access to banking services, irrespective of their location. It is an extension of Internet banking. Various types of services are provided by mobile banking such as account balance mobile alerts about credit card or debit card transactions, mini account statement etc.
8. Door Step Banking: Here, the customer is not required to visit the bank for obtaining services or products from the bank. This means banking services and products are provided to a customer at his residence or workplace.
9. Point Of Sale (POS) : Using a debit or credit card purchases being made is point of sales as mentioned above the process wherein the card have to be swiped.
10. ATMs: These are very useful and easier means which ensure dispensing of cash at anytime, anywhere. ATMs are self service kiosks and are like cash

vending machines which help the banks to provide banking services to customers at convenient locations.

11. Virtual Banking: Rendering or banking services through use of technology. Most important types of services which come under virtual banking are electronic fund transfer, phone banking, credit card, internet banking, debit card, etc.

12. Electronic Clearing Services (ECS): Electronic mode of transfer from one bank to another automatically is ECS.

Figure: 3.1 The Indian Financial Structure

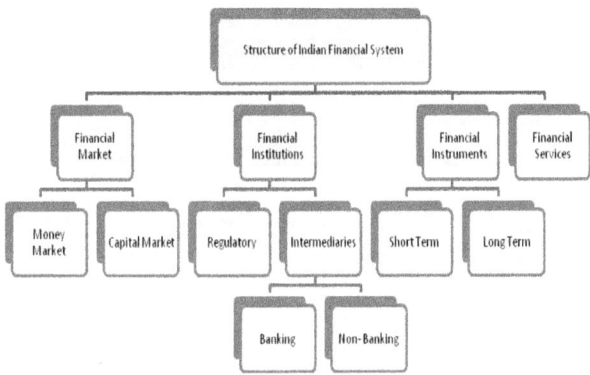

Source: Compiled by researcher from the available literature

The Structure of Indian Financial system is comprised of Financial Markets which is distributed into Money Market and Capital Market, and then there are Financial Institutions which are of two types Regulatory and Intermediaries, which can be of again two types Banking Intermediaries and Non- banking intermediaries. Financial instruments are also part of Indian Financial System which could be of Short term nature or Long term. There are other financial services which come in the purview of Indian Financial system.

This banking part is again explained through a banking structure which covers all the banking services performed by the banking institutions in India.

Figure 3.2: Banking Activities Performance

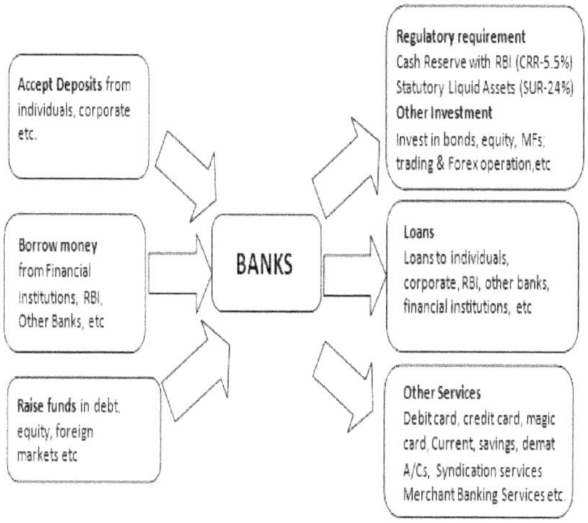

```
Accept Deposits from
individuals, corporate
etc.                              Regulatory requirement
                                  Cash Reserve with RBI (CRR-5.5%)
                                  Statutory Liquid Assets (SLR-24%)
                                  Other Investment
                                  Invest in bonds, equity, MFs;
                                  trading & Forex operation, etc

Borrow money
from Financial          BANKS     Loans
Institutions, RBI,                Loans to individuals,
Other Banks, etc                  corporate, RBI, other banks,
                                  financial institutions, etc

Raise funds in debt,              Other Services
equity, foreign                   Debit card, credit card, magic
markets etc                       card, Current, savings, demat
                                  A/Cs, Syndication services
                                  Merchant Banking Services etc.
```

Source: Compiled by researcher from the available literature

The various activities performed by the banks are accepting deposits from individuals and corporate, borrow money from financial institutions, RBI and other banks, raise funds in debt, equity, foreign markets, etc. Maintaining reserves as per the regulatory requirement of RBI as per the required Cash Reserve Ratio and Statutory Liquidity Ratio, providing loans to individuals, corporate, etc. and providing other financial services like debit card, credit card, current and savings accounts, demat accounts, and other such services.

At this point it is important to know about the structure of the Indian Banking System and the different types of banks and other banking services.

3.3 The Indian Banking System

Figure: 3.3: Structure of Indian Banking System

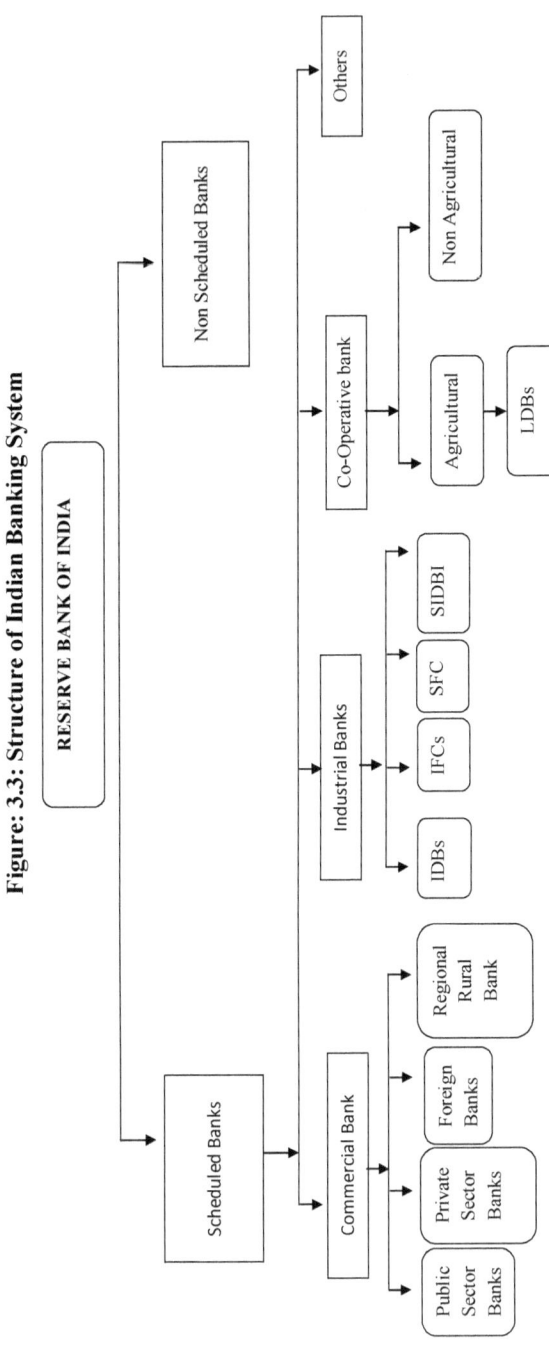

Source: Compiled by researcher from the available literature

The Indian financial system is comprised of cooperative banks and commercial banks, specialised developmental banks for agriculture, industry, external trade, social security institutions, collective investment institutions, etc. And banking is the main part of the financial system.

RBI is the apex of the Indian banking system. All the commercial banks come under the RBI, including private and public, foreign banks, local banks also regional rural banks and co operative banks.

The banking industry in India is highly regulated. Few important regulations are mentioned below:

1. Accept deposits from individuals and corporate, etc.
2. Borrow money from financial institutions, RBI, Other banks, etc.
3. Raise funds in debt, equity, foreign markets, etc.(CRR-5.5%),
4. Regulatory Requirement like Cash Reserve with RBI, maintain Statutory Liquidity Reserve of 24%.
5. Other Investments in bonds, equity, Mutual Funds, etc.
6. Loans to individuals and corporate.
7. Other Services.

Banks are earning incomes by lending money at interest and by charging fee for services they render. Banks charge for every service rendered by them be it an electronic transfer or payments through Internet banking system.

Commercial banks

They are the banks which deal in commercial banking operations like acceptance of deposits, sanctioning loans to the public.

Commercial banks are classified into Scheduled & Non-Scheduled Banks.

A) Scheduled banks

A bank that is listed under the second schedule of the RBI Act, 1934 is known as Scheduled Bank. Scheduled Banks are generally private, foreign and nationalized banks operating in India. However, even cooperative banks are allowed to enjoy the status of scheduled banks if they suit certain criteria. A scheduled bank is entitled to get loans from the RBI at the bank rate. They have membership to clearing houses. Further the scheduled banks are classified into:

1. Nationalized schedule commercial banks
2. Foreign banks
3. Other non-nationalized scheduled banks

Non Scheduled Bank

Those banks whose names do not appear in the second schedule of RBI Act 1934 is a Non Scheduled Bank. Such a bank is not bound to perform banking services according to the policies and instructions of the RBI.

Commercial banks are further classified into:

i) **Public Sector Banks:** The banks which are controlled by the government is a public sector bank. All the nationalized banks and regional rural banks are public sector banks like State Bank and its subsidiaries, Syndicate Bank, Canara Bank, Bank of Baroda, etc. The public sector banks in India emerged to its current form in three stages. Firstly, there was conversion of the Imperial Bank of India into the state bank of India in 1955 as mentioned before, followed by the taking over of the seven state associated banks, second the nationalization of 14 major commercial banks on July 19, 1969 and lastly, the nationalization of 6 more commercial banks on April 15, 1980. Thus 27 banks constitute the Public sector in Indian commercial banking.

ii) Private Sector Bank: These banks are owned and controlled by private institutions or individuals and not by the government. For example, ICICI Bank, HDFC Bank, Axis Bank, etc. In January 2001, RBI issued new rules for the licensing of new banks in the private sector. Eg-A new bank may be started with a capital of Rs 200 crore. The net worth is to be raised to Rs 300 crore in three years. The promoter's minimum holding in the capital shall be 40 per cent with a lock-in-period of 5 years. Excess holding over 40 per cent will have to be diluted within a year. Non-resident Indians can pick up 40 per cent equity share in the new bank. Any foreign bank or finance company may join as technical collaborators or as co-promoter, but their equity participation will be restricted to 20 per cent, which will be within the ceiling of 40 per cent allowed to Non resident India. Corporates have been allowed to invest up to meet existing priority sector norms and prudential norms and also to open 25 % of their branches in rural and semi-urban areas. Preference will be given to promoters with expertise in financing priority areas and rural and agro based industries. Non-banking finance companies may convert themselves into banks if their net worth is Rs. 200 crore, capital adequacy ratio is 12%, non performing assets below 5% and possess triple A credit rating. In addition to the above guidelines, the new banks are governed by the provisions of the Reserve Bank of India Act, the Banking Regulation Act and other relevant statutes.

iii) Foreign Banks: These banks have a registration in foreign countries and their head office is in a foreign location and has opened branches in India like HSBC Bank, Standard Chartered Bank, Citibank, etc. These banks have to get a license from the RBI and for granting the same the RBI has to look for certain factors like whether the banks are financially sound, their ranking in international rating and in their country. The relationship between their home country and India. There should be constant supervision of the foreign banks' home country, and the minimum required capital is 25 million US$ which is spread in three branches 10 million $ for first two branches and 5 million US$ for the third one.

iv) Regional Rural Banks (RRB):

Establishment of RRBs was by Regional Rural Banks Act, 1976 for providing banking services to the rural people. For Example: Allahabad UP Gramin Bank, Andhra Pradesh Grameen Bikas Bank, Uttarakhand Gramin Bank, etc. RRBs are new banking firms that supplement the banking done by co operative and commercial banks in serving the rural sector. These banks were set up in October 1975 under the Regional Rural Bank Act, 1976. As of now there are 196 RRBs which function in 484 districts. RRBs are related with commercial banks as they give the proposal for the establishment of RRB and known as sponsor bank. The RBI establishes an RRB on the proposal of the sponsor bank and then the local limits are then specified pertaining to its branches and agencies.

Work of a Regional Rural Bank

An RRB is involved in banking business which is the business of banking which is also defined in section 5(b) of the Banking Regulation Act, 1949 and is engaged in one or more forms of businesses as specific in Section 6 (1) of the Act. An RRB may take up following businesses:

1. It can grant loans and advances to small farmers, labourers in agriculture, for agriculture and allied activities.

2. It can grant loans to small businessmen, small traders, small producers within the specified rural areas.

V) Development Banks An industrial bank is a bank that grants loans to individuals and companies that are associated with specific industry types and have a limited scope of services. They cater to small businesses and industries. **IFCI**, earlier known as **Industrial Finance Corporation of India**, is an Indian government owned development bank to provide service to the long-term finance needs of the industrial sector. It was the first of its kind Development Financial Institution established by the government of India after independence.

(IDBI) The Industrial Development Bank of India was established as a wholly owned subsidiary of the RBI in 1964 under the Act of Parliament. The ownership of IDBI got transferred to the Government in 1976 and had been made the financial institution for the coordination of activities of institutions which were engaged in developing, financing, and promoting industries in India.

IDBI was providing assistance in finance in foreign and Indian currencies for expansion, diversification, modernisation and green field projects.

IDBI provided financial assistance, both in Indian and foreign currencies, for green-field projects and also for expansion, modernisation and diversification purposes. IDBI was also providing financial assistance indirectly by refinancing the loans granted by State level financial institutions or banks by rediscounting bills of exchange which arose from sale of indigenous machinery on which payment was deferred.

Small Industries Development Bank of India (SIDBI) is an independent financial institution aimed to help in the development of micro, small and medium-scale enterprises was integrated initially as a wholly owned subsidiary of Industrial

Development Bank of India. As of now the ownership is held by 34 Government of India owned and controlled institutions. It began its operations as a refinancing agency to banks and state level financial institutions for providing credit to small scale industries, since then there have been expansion in its activities, including direct credit to the SME sector through its 100 branches in almost all major industrial areas in the country. It also plays a developmental role by supporting micro finance institutions for capacity enhancement and lending. There have been seven Micro finance branches opened by SIDBI aimed in disbursing loans up to Rs. 5 lakhs.

Land Development Banks- The Land Development banks were registered under the Multi State Co-operative Societies Act, with a mandate to act as financing for investment for agriculture development project. The basic financing is done for creation of various resources for irrigation, farm machines, etc.

Cooperative Banks

There are co-operative societies that are formed at a state or district level and have a share of more than 51%. These are set up for the purpose of services to the farming community or to aid in land or infrastructure development at the state or district level. They are of two types:

1. Non Agricultural Banks: These banks are primarily located in urban or semi urban areas. Such banks could only lend money for non agricultural purposes till 1996. Now the distinction has been removed. They lent to small businesses and small borrowers. For Example: Ahmadabad Mercantile Co-op Bank, Kalupur Commercial Co-op Bank.

2. Agricultural Banks: They are the apex co-operative bank in a state and monitor all the financial activities of all the co-operative banks in the state. For example: Kerala State Co-operative Bank, West Bengal State Co-operative

Bank. NABARD (National Bank for Agriculture and Rural Development): NABARD was established as an apex bank that renders finance for agriculture and rural development specifically.

v) **Others**

Indigenous Bankers-

Indigenous bankers comprise of the earliest form of banking system in the country. They had carried on the old system of operations of banking in India using different nomenclature. Like in Chennai, such bankers are called Chettys ; in Northern India Sahukars, Mahajans and Khatnes; in Mumbai, Shroffs and Marwaris; and in Bengal, Seths and Banias. As per the Indian Central Banking Enquiry Committee, has defined indigenous banker as a firm or individual which is receiving deposits, dealing in hundies or engaging in money lending.

There can be three types of Indigenous bankers:

(a) dealing in business of banking for example Multani bankers.

(b) combining business of banking with trade like Marwaris.

(c) Dealing in trade and having limited business of banking.

There is a difference in indigenous banker and money lender the money lender is actually not a banker as he lends his own funds while an indigenous banker lends and accepts funds from people.

Chit Funds

Chit funds are a form of savings scheme prevalent in India. It is a firm which conducts, manages or supervises such a fund, it can be better understood by going through the definition in Section 2(b) of the Chit Fund Act, 1982:

"Chit means a transaction whether called chit, chit fund, chitty, kuree or by any other name by or under which a person enters into an agreement with a specified number of persons that every one of them shall subscribe a certain sum of money (or a certain quantity of grain instead) by way of periodical installments over a definite period and that each such subscriber shall, in his turn, as determined by lot or by auction or by tender or in such other manner as may be specified in the chit agreement, be entitled to the prize amount"

Such kinds of schemes can be conducted either by organized financial institutions or unorganized schemes conducted informally amongst relatives. Some chit funds are made for some specific purposes. In Kerala chit funds had played a pivotal role in providing credit to all sections of the society. Kerala State Financial Enterprise under the Kerala Government is mainly doing business of chit funds.

The Banking System of India is entirely based on interest that is the scheduled banks or non scheduled banks, industrial banks. As these banking and non banking institutions are based on the Banking Regulation Act and other acts which have a component of interest and also as per banks:

- As per the Section 5 (b) and 5 (c) of the Banking Regulation Act banks are prohibited to make an investment on the basis of Profit and Loss Sharing which is one of the bases of Islamic banking.
- As per the Banking Regulations Act (BR Act, 1949) Section 8 reads, "No banking company shall directly or indirectly deal in buying or selling or bartering of goods…"
- As per the Banking Regulation Act Section 9 it is prohibited to use any immovable property except for private use- which is against the condition of Ijarah which is meant for home finance.

- As per Banking Regulations Act Section 21 payment of interest is required which is against the principle of Islamic law.

The various banking and financial institutions working in India are functioning on the principles of interest based banking. In such an environment, there is an immense potential for starting interest free banking. Thus, it is important for introduction of Islamic Banking in India through Non Banking Finance Companies or by inserting a clause in the present banking rules and regulations.

After the discussion of the evolution of banking system in India and the development taking place in Indian banking system, the next chapter presents the concept and global practices related to Islamic banking with a view to find out the possibilities of introduction of interest free banking in the present interest based Indian banking system.

CHAPTER-4

ISLAMIC BANKING: CONCEPT AND GLOBAL PRACTICES

The present chapter explains the concept of the financial and banking system in Sharia in Islam and gives the view of its practices in different countries of the world.

4.1 Concept of Islamic Banking

As explained in Chapter 1 the concept of Islamic Banking is not a new one and was practiced at the time of Prophet (pbuh) and also at the time of different Caliphs who had taken the reins of Islamic dynasty.

Islamic Banking is a system of banking which functions as per the rules of Sharia (Islamic Law) as per which riba (interest) is prohibited in financial transactions. According to Islam one cannot earn money with money as this leads to exploitation of the masses and inequality in the society. In actual practice in India if a person is in need of money he approaches a bank, he will be funded but he has to pay principal amount and interest amount both which is divided in monthly or yearly instalments, so the total sum of money which he is paying to the bank is generally quite high. This practice leads to rich becoming richer and poor becoming poorer and thus results in inequality in the society. For this particular reason interest is prohibited in Islam because riba in Islamic shariah considered as a tool of oppression and a medium to get the other's money by exploiting his/her needs and situations. Hence, Islam forbids a system based on riba (interest) and it promotes charity works alternatively. "And their taking of Riba (usury) though they were forbidden from taking it and their devouring of men's substance wrongfully (bribery, etc.). And we have prepared for the disbelievers among them a painful torment". Quran 4:161 [Al-Nisa]

It is also important to mention about Islamic Development Bank which is responsible for the functioning of Islamic banks worldwide and is engaged in various social functions of the community.

The Islamic Development Bank (IDB) is a financial institution of international repute and was founded in the wake of Declaration of Intent which was issued in the Jeddah Conference of Muslim Countries held in December 1973. This conference was attended by finance ministers of most of the Muslim countries. The first meeting of the board of governors of the bank took place in July 1975 and the bank came in to existence in 20 October1975.

Purpose of establishment

The main objective of IDB is to promote the growth of Muslim communities of member countries economically and socially at individual level and jointly according to Sharia i.e. Islamic Law.

Functions of IDB

The main functions of Islamic Development Bank are to contribute in capital generation and to funding loans for constructive project works and for entrepreneurs also besides giving financial help to its member nations in other ways for social and economic development. The Bank also establishes and operates special funds for special objectives including a fund base to help Muslim communities of non-member countries, in addition for setting up different trust funds. The Bank can also receive deposits for mobilizing financial resources through Shariah compatible laws. It also has an obligation to assist member countries in the endorsement of foreign trade especially in capital goods, among member countries; it provides technical support to member countries; and extends training programs for human resources occupied in developmental programs in Muslim member countries to conform to the Sharia.

Membership

At present, 56 countries are member of Islamic Development Bank. The primary condition to be a member of this bank is that the prospective country must be a member of Organisation of Islamic Cooperation (OIC), pay its part to capital of the Bank and must be willing to accept terms and conditions as may be decided upon by governors of Board the bank.

Capital

Decisions about the authorized capital and subscribed capital were taken in the 38th Annual Meet of the Board of Governors; and it was decided that authorized capital of the IDB will be raised to ID 100 billion and subscribed capital to ID 50 billion.

Head Office and Regional Offices

The Bank's head office is in the city of Jeddah in the Kingdom of Saudi Arabia (KSA). There are four regional offices of the bank were opened in Rabat (Morocco, 1994), Kuala Lumpur (Malaysia, 1994), Almaty (Kazakhstan, 1997) and Dakar (Senegal, 2008). Bank also has two country gateway offices one in Ankara (Turkey) and another one in Jakarta (Indonesia) and 14 field representatives in 14 member countries respectively in "Afghanistan, Azerbaijan, Bangladesh, Burkina Faso, Guinea, Iran, Mali, Pakistan, Sudan, Turkmenistan, Uzbekistan, Yemen, Mauritania and Libya". The Bank's financial year is according to lunar Hijri Year.

4.2 Financial Contracts in Islamic Finance

Some basic financing contracts in compliance with Sharia have been developed for Islamic Banks. The Islamic financing system broadly, is based on two principles viz profit-loss sharing and Marginal (non-PLS). Profit-loss sharing includes Mudarba (trustee finance) and Musharka (equity participation) while Marginal(non-pls) draws upon mark up principle. These principles are having a bearing on assets and liabilities of a bank. (Zaher and Hassan, 2001), (Sundararajan and Errico, 2002)

1) **Murabaha (cost plus sale)** In a murabaha agreement it is a cost plus profit contract in which the bank purchases the asset on the request of the client then it is sold to the customer on a deferred payment basis with a margin or mark-up.

2) **Musharaka (partnership or joint venture)**

   This kind of contract is usually for long term investment projects. It is a form of participation contract. Here the customer also invests some of his own capital and this type of a venture is known as Musharka. It is a contact based on PLS system and the profits are shared according to the pre agreed terms and losses are borne as per investment.

3) **Mudaraba (trustee finance contract)**

   Under this agreement, the Islamic Bank provides the total capital requisite for an investment project, and its customer (or entrepreneur) makes contributions in form of labor and expertise. As it is a PLS agreement, the profits from the project are shared between the concerned bank and the customer in a fixed proportion. The losses, raised from investments are borne entirely by the bank, while the customer is only liable to invest his time and efforts for this cause. But if circumstances prove that losses on investments have arisen due to negligence of customer then in such a situation the customer is held responsible for the losses and hence he is made to bear the losses raised from investments

A Mudaraba contract is shown on both sides of the balance sheet of a bank. On the liability side, the contract between the bank and the depositors is known as unrestricted Mudaraba in which the depositors agree that their funds is to be used by the bank's discretion, to finance an open-ended list (unrestricted) of profitable investments and expect to share with the bank the overall profits accrued and earned.

4) **Ijara (leasing contract)**

Ijara is somewhat similar to a conventional operating lease, where an Islamic bank (lessor) leases assets to a customer (lessee) with an agreed lease payments for a specified maturity, but it does not entitle ownership to the customer (lessee). On the contrary, under Ijara wa Iqtina' which is similar to the conventional financial or capital lease, where the Islamic bank (lessor) finances assets such as building, equipments or business projects and leases it to the customer for an agreed lease rental payment, besides this the customer agrees to make lease payments towards purchase of the asset from the lessor by the end of the leasing period. Zaher and Hassan (2001) mentioned in their study that many investors, especially Islamic banks, have been inclined towards Islamic leasing with the promise of higher yields than Murabaha, which accounts for the bulk of Islamic banks financial contracts.

5) **Istisna (a lease contract)**

Istisna is usually employed in finance of manufacturing or establishment of plant, projects, houses, roads, bridges, highways, etc. It is a sale contract under which the transaction of the commodity takes place before its production. When the manufacturer agrees to manufacture the product as specified by the customer then the contract of Istisna takes place. An important aspect for the validity of Istisna'a is that the price is agreed with the consent of the parties taking into account the specifications of the commodity (intended to be manufactured).

6) **Qard-e-hasan (benevolent loans)**

Islamic banks provide such a facility with a zero return loan and charge the borrowers only service fee to cover the administrative expenses for handling the loan. Such loans are negative net present value investments to Islamic banks and are confined to the poor sections of society such as needy students or small rural farmers.

7) **Joalah (service charge)**

This mode usually applies to transactions such as consultations and professional services, funds placements and trust services. It refers to a situation when a party undertakes to pay another party a specified amount of money as a fee for rendering services as per the terms and conditions of the contract.

8) **Bai Muajjal (credit sale or deferred payment sale)**

Credit sales or deferred payment sale, in which the seller can sell a product on the basis of deferred payment in instalments or in a lump sum payments. The price of the product is agreed upon between the buyer and the seller at the time of the sale and cannot include any charge for deferring payments. Islamic banks can add a certain percentage to the purchase price or additional costs associated with the transaction as a profit margin, and the purchased product/asset will serve as a guarantee to the bank.

9) **Bai salam or bai salaf (future sales contract or purchase with deferred delivery)**

It is sale of a article of trade where the buyer pays the seller the full agreed price of the said article, and in return the seller promises to deliver the product at some specified future date. The specifications of the commodity to be sold must be negotiated and mentioned in the contract.

10) **Takaful**

In an abstract manner, takaful is believed as mutual insurance, in which participants add a fixed amount of funds to a common pool of funds. The objective of this system is not to make profits and returns, but to work on the principle of "bear one another's burden". The main beliefs of takaful system are:

a) Policyholders collaborate with each other for their common welfare.

b) Policy holders' contributions are perceived as grants to the pool of funds.

c) Every policyholder makes her subscription to assist those people who need support.

d) Losses are divided and liabilities distributed in accordance with the society pooling system.

e) Risk is diversified and hence reduced concerned with subscription and compensation.

f) It does not produce benefits at the expense of others members.

Muslim academicians have "hardly any difference of opinion" on "the need for managing, redeeming and mitigating general, business and life risks covered by the insurance business." But whether conventional insurance is forbidden (haram) is an argument.

Views on Conventional Insurance

Orthodox Islamic academics opined that Commercial insurance is not permitted for Muslim people as it includes Al-Gharar (uncertainty), Al-Maisir (gambling), Riba (usury). There are basically two areas of concerns regarding conventional system of insurance. The uncertainty or risks "if and when the insured event will take place and, if it does take place, what would be the relationship of compensation to the insurance premium paid". What if the policyholder of accidental insurance never has a motor vehicle accident? The policyholders lose and the insurance firm wins. Regarding life insurance, every individual dies, but what if the death occurs after the payment of first premium? The policyholders win and the insurance firm loses. This "makes the insurance business similar to gambling, where the gambler does not know the fate of the game." Thus, uncertainty in the conventional insurance business "is excessive and borders on prohibited gharar."

"Insurance companies invest surplus funds on the basis of interest and pay out a part of such earnings to policyholders as bonuses". As per the "orthodox interpretation", this is riba.

Arguments for Takaful

Islamic intellectuals advocate takaful with reference to [Quran 5:2] and various Hadiths of Prophet Muhammad ☐ some of them are worth to be mentioned.

Quran

Basis of Co-operation: Assist each other in al-Birr and in al-Taqwa (virtue, righteousness and piousness), but do not help each other in committing evil acts and wrongdoing. (Sūrah al-Mā'idah, Verse 2)[Quran 5:2]

Hadith

"Allah will always grant His mercy upon his devotees for as long as they help others."(Narration by Imam Ahmad bin Hanbal and Imam Abu Daud.)

Basis of Responsibility: "The place of relationships and feelings of people with faith, between each other, is just like the body; when one of its parts is afflicted with pain, then the rest of the body will be affected". (Narratives by Imam al-Bukhari and Imam Muslim)

"One true Muslim (Mu'min) and another true Muslim are like a building, whereby every part in it strengthens the other part." (Narratives by Imam al-Bukhari and Imam Muslim)

Basis of Mutual Protection: "By my life (which is in God's power), nobody will enter Paradise if he does not protect his neighbour who is in distress". (Narrative of Imam Ahmad bin Hanbal.) The fundamentals underlying takaful are very similar to co-operative and mutual principles, to the extent that the co-operative and mutual model is one that is accepted under Islamic law.

Takaful Industry and Models

Historical Prespective

The history of Islam gives the concept of takaful which was reportedly been practised in quite a number of ways since 622 AD. Many Muslim scholars have acknowledged the basis of shared responsibility or mutual insurance was practiced in earlier times in Mecca and Madina.

There were difference in opinions regarding the legitimacy of takaful and some scholars stated that it is basically "Islamisizing of conventional insurance". It was in 1976 when a fatwa issued by the Higher Council of Saudi Arabia in favour of Islamic model of insurance. The first Takaful Company was started in Sudan named as The

Islamic Insurance Company in 1979, and by mid 1990s the number of Takaful companies increased to seven in Sudan, Dubai Saudi Arabia, Bahrain and Jordan. The Takaful industry has been growing since then and as of 2013 the leading countries in takaful business are Malaysia and the Gulf countries.

4.3 Islamic Finance Pattern in India

Nisar Shariq (n.d.) mentioned a brief account of work on Islamic finance in India since the beginning of the twentieth century. This work may be broadly categorized as theoretical and/or practical. The literature gives reflections on different aspects of economics, zakah and population. The concrete efforts undertaken by members of the Islamic community were aimed at setting up institutions which provide either interest free or minimum cost loans to Muslim people.

From a practical perspective, efforts of a prominent person an 'alim of Hyderabad can be traced back to the 1890s when he established an organisation named as "Anjuman Mowudul Ikhwyn". This organisation was mainly a welfare association which used to collect donations and skins of dead animals at the time of Eid ul adha from the public in order to provide interest free loans to the marginal section of society. By the end of year 1944, this organization's assets were accounted for Rs. 15,000 and simultaneously it had sanctioned loans of approximately Rs. 600,000.

There were twelve similar organizations came into existence and few of these organisations were functioning till the Partition of India took place.

There was another organisation set up in 1923 by the workers and employees of the department of Land Development (Makama-I bandubast wa dkhila uqaqal-ardi). Within twenty years of its establishment, this organization owned assets, worth Rs. 100,000, reserves Rs.3000 and had been sanctioning loans of Rs. 5,000-6,000 per month. In 1944 there were around 1,000 members (Muslims and non-Muslims) of this society

In the western part of India, an organisation "Patni Co-operative Credit Society", Surat (Gujarat), was established in 1939, with an authorized capital of Rs.15000 in order to provide interest-free loans to its members. This society has been functioning till now and use to provide interest-free loans to its members that too without any collateral security or service charges. In order to meet its operational expenses the society used to operate a consumers cooperative store, which later on was wound up because of the heavy losses it sustained. By the end of year 1997-98, the society had a reserve fund of Rs. 3,761,800.6.

The Muslim Fund Tanda Baoli, set up in 1940, Rampur, north India was also functioning in a well manner. But the partition of India had a devastating effect on the functioning and further formation of such societies for a very long period. Many societies including Muslim Fund Tanda Baoli were forced to be wound up due to Partition (mass eruption of riots, and the migration of the upper economic classes to Pakistan) and bad loans.

In 1961, The Muslim Fund Deoband (MFD) was established, and has been functioning since its establishment. Tar Bayt al-Mal Hyderabad was next to be set up in 1966. Besides this, Muslim Fund Najibabad (MFN) was also established on the similar pattern of MFD in 1971. (Nisar, 2004)

Muslims also started getting into profit oriented business by 1980s. The reason being for this participation was mainly by that time Muslims also had obtained some financial knowledge as they were engaged in non profit businesses, second there was a movement which empowered Muslims all over the world and lastly the policy of

LPG that is liberalization, privatization and globalization in the economy provided newer opportunities for growth of businesses.

The NBFC which first started in 1980 working on Islamic values was known as Al-Mizan in Madras which was basically a group of small partnership firms involved in leather business. Their effort could not survive for long and by 1984-85 it came to an end. Since then there have been some NBFCs of which a note can be made of like:

1. BIG Barkat Investment Group 1983
2. Al-Amin Islamic Financial & Investment Corporation of India 1986
3. Al-Barr Finance House Ltd. 1989
4. Syed Shariyat Finance 1989
5. Assalam Finance & Investment Ltd. 1990
6. Baitul Islam Finance Ltd. 1990

BIG that is the Barkat Investment Group has one of the most performing Islamic financial institutions in India. It came into existence with the merger of two firms that is Falah Investments Ltd and Ittefaq Investments Ltd in 1988 which were floated by BUN(Baitun Nasr Co-operative Society) as BUN was not allowed to make investments. And in 1991 BLFSL was also formed by Barkat that is Barkat Leasing and Financial Services Ltd. And has seen a notable growth in its funds like funds under its management had seen an increase from Rs.1.6 million in March 1989 to Rs.270 million in March 1997 which is tremendous growth in a period of eight years. Its returns to depositors also remained in positive that is between 10-25% in these years as can be seen from Table 4.1

Due to limited options for business that is trading only in stocks and real estate one of the schemes incurred losses of 8.56 lakhs in 1995-96 and 5.85 lakhs in 1996-97 in Stocks in Return to depositors. All the schemes of Barkat made losses of about 25%

in the year 1997-98. The total loss incurred to the company was amounting to Rs.32.8 million and after two years Barkat was finally closed by the government in May 2000. The major reason for its losses had been investment in real estate and stocks and due to the slump in the market in 1995 and realty market hit by unprecedented recession caused to its further losses and led to closure in the year 2000.

Table 4.1 Financial Performance of Barkat Investment Group (1988-1998 in Lakhs)

Year	1988-89	1989-90	1990-91	1991-92	1992-93	1993-94	1994-95	1995-96	1996-97	1997-98
Gross Profit	8.88	13.141	27.833	56.512	79.358	158.76	286.378	313.433	401.241	-60.356
Expenses	5.131	6.7	7.478	15.766	26.777	48.78	104.178	149.457	432.456	257.326
Net Profit	3.749	6.441	20.355	40.746	52.581	109.98	182.2	163.98	168.79	-317.68
Depositors Share	1.874	4.831	15.267	30.56	42.065	93.29	150.373	139.857	253.225	27.969
Deposits Mobilized	9.865	27.65	85.96	151.58	262.317	567.75	970.664	1807.027	2262.484	1135.38

Return to Depositors

BIC	19	17.5	17.75	20	16	16.25	14	12	10	-25.45
Stocks						25	14	-8.56	-5.85	-25.45
Leasing					6	13.64	15.23	15	10.45	0
Retained Fund	1.875	1.61	5.088	10.186	10.516	16.69	31.827	24.119	-84.44	-345.651
Add less retained Fund b/d	0	1.875	3.485	8.573	18.759	29.275	45.965	77.792	101.911	17.471
Net Retained Fund	1.875	3.485	8.573	18.759	29.275	45.965	77.792	101.91	17.471	-328.18

Source: Nisar,S, Islamic Non Banking Financial Institutions in India: Special Focus on Regulation (2004)

BLFSL The leasing company of Barkat had worked in the entire period except for the year 1997-98 when the net return on working capital came down by 7.23% and its net return to investment came down to 6.99%. It was the year in which major regulatory changes in April 1997 had occurred in NBFCs in India, as per which the firms involved in investment activities were banned in accepting any new deposits. So there had been major issues in terms of liquidity, other NBFCs could resort to other means for meeting out its liquidity requirements but Barkat as committed to Sharia could not resort to such ventures. And no such assistance came to Barkat either in the country or outside and this led to closure of one of the promising Islamic NBFC in India in May 2000. Nisar (2004)

Baitun Nasr Urban Cooperative Credit Society (BUN)

BUN was started on trial in 1973 and got regularized in 1976 as an Urban Cooperative Credit Society under the Maharashtra Cooperative Credit Societies Act. Its main purpose was to provide banking services to its members on an interest free basis and extended credit on actual service charge only. Table 4.2 gives a glimpse of its financial performance from 1977 to 1999. BUN was closed due to its association with the Barkat Group. As Nisar (2004) suggested that BUN was not closed down for its bad investments as it was not allowed to do any investments but on the basis of its association with the Barkat Group. In the period of its existence the number of branches grew to 20 in Mumbai, the number of members increased from 654 to 155050.

The lending by BUN was secured by gold, silver and property. To keep up pace with the advancement of technology it had a scientific system of calculation of service charges and all its 20 branches were computerized. The depositors of the firm did not take the case to the court and till date the society has been dormant.

Table 4.2 Financial Performance of Baitun Nasr (1997-99)

Share capital, Total Deposits, Loan Turnover and Total Assets are in '000

Years	1977	1982	1987	1992	1997	1998	1999
Branches	1	4	7	12	18	18	20
Members	654	6820	20356	47186	120510	137797	155050
Share Capital	26	126	584	2862	13035	12993	12762
Total Deposits	36	171	6191	26302	108580	119184	124159
Loan Turnover	49	3062	15977	58088	278995	324950	364810
Total Assets	0	13	705	5497	25760	30405	34598

Source: Nisar,S, Islamic Non Banking Financial Institutions in India: Special Focus on Regulation (2004)

Al-Najib Milli Mutual Benefits Limited (AMMB)

This is another financial institution managed by Muslims and has 41 branches in the northern part of India and has deposits of over Rs. 200 million. As far adherence to Sharia is concerned it is not clear of its operations and cannot be termed as Islamic financial institution.

The Muslim Fund Najibabad (MFN) had floated AMMB in 1993. As AMMB was a Mutual Benefit Finance Company under section 620 A of the NON Banking Financial Companies Act, hence the new regulations was not applicable directly on it.

AMMB had another advantage of moving flexibly between MFN the parent organization and AMMB as the group was the same. Due to this operational flexibility the group was able to counteract some of the regulatory changes that might have affected its business prospects.

Also the AMMB follows a policy of keeping its major part of its deposits with commercial banks, which provided a source of revenue. Table 4.3 shows the financial performance of AMMB which is being stronger.

Table 4.3: Financial Performance of Al-Najib Milli Mutual Benefits Limited (1993-99) (Figures in Rs. '000)

Year	Deposits	Loan	Investments	Profit after Tax
1993	53,635.44	28,623.45	352.60	2.18
1994	66,953.61	37,306.80	1072.60	3.55
1995	91,050.83	44,834.90	1339.20	34.07
1996	112,307.37	53,401.38	1674.90	29.54
1997	120,763.01	66,568.84	1874.50	52.18
1998	140,330.79	72922.46	5660.15	96.41
1999	161,718.97	78,062.76	16495.65	103.63
2000	193,285.05	80,518.04	15875.50	51.71

Source: Nisar,S, Islamic Non Banking Financial Institutions in India: Special Focus on Regulation (2004)

Al-Barr Finance House Ltd. (ABFL)

Earlier it was known as Al-Baraka Finance House Ltd. and was supported by Dallah Al Baraka Group in 1989. This was the only Islamic financial institution backed up by a foreign group. During 1990s it was majorly unknown to public and it was by 1998 when new policies had come up it succeeded in stepping up in its activities. It is registered under the NBFCs Act. It had a fewer number of branches with small public deposits and had a foreign holding of 51%, this approach of ABFL made it progress slowly but steadily.

Table 4.4 shows the financial performance of the company from the period 1990 to 1998.

The major part of the firm's resources is invested in short term Murabahah and during emergency it can approach commercial institutions too. From the table 4.4 it is evident that the total income increased from 12 lakhs in 1990 to 715 lakhs by 1999. The company distributed dividend at the rate of 12%.

Table 4.4: Financial Highlights of Al-Barr Finance House Ltd. (1990-1999)
(Figures in Rs. 100,000)

Year	1990	1991	1992	1993	1994	1995	1996	1997	1998	1999
Total Income	12.43	15.66	85.65	145.34	186.93	288.26	434.65	604.39	657.59	715.21
Profit	0.06	2.92	17.39	41.29	45.98	100.02	115.92	106.33	80.44	85.23
Dividend		14	15	12	10	11	12	12	12	12
Fixed Assets	0.38	0.75	45.72	180.60	193.82	433.53	743.55	959.56	1232.35	1197.18
Share Capital	15.00	21.56	300.00	300.00	400.00	400.00	400.00	430.00	430.00	430.00
Reserves and Surplus	0.06	0.60	5.15	12.87	25.17	81.19	149.10	233.18	261.26	289.40

Source: Nisar,S, Islamic Non Banking Financial Institutions in India: Special Focus on Regulation (2004)

From the period of 1980-1990 there were surge of Islamic NBFCs in India. But due to large scale regulatory changes in the non banking sector did have a bad effect on the NBFC sector. Islamic NBFCs suffered more due to their adherence to Sharia and not comprising on the values even in conditions of crises. The other factors which contributed to the failure of Islamic NBFCs were lack of lender of the last resort, inexperienced attitude towards the regulations, risk associated with Islamic financial institutions, etc. For overcoming such failure more experience, alertness and informed investors, proper training, updated technology is required to tackle such a situation.

In August 2013, the RBI had permitted a firm in Kerala to operate as an NBFC that is based on Islamic principles, which is a small step towards developing Sharia compliant finance in India. There are now over 12,000 registered non-banking financial companies registered in India today. Most Sharia compliant investment and business in India occurs through the NBFCs. In August 2013, a Sharia compliant financial institution was established by Cheraman Financial Services Limited (CFSL) with Kerala State Industrial Development Corporation (KSIDC) being the single largest shareholder, holding 11% shares. CFSL has already received clearances from the RBI, the Security and Exchange Board of India and the Wakf Board. CFSL will engage in the infrastructure, services, and manufacturing sectors and has an initial capital of INR 1,000 crore (Majeethia and Bose, 2014). It has already funded start-ups and infrastructure projects and floated the Rs 2.5bn Cheramun Fund, a private equity fund with a minimum of Rs 10 million set by the Securities and Exchange Board of India (SEBI) per investor. It has a subsidiary, Cheramun Infrastructure, which channels ethical developments to developing world class industrial infrastructure in Kerala (Arab News, 2014). Thus, Shariah compliant finance is occurring on a small scale through non-banking financial companies and law firms in India. However, in order to operate full-fledged Islamic banks and Islamic windows, an amendment to the Banking Regulation Act 1949 may be required. Alternatively, India may consider creating a completely separate sector for Islamic banking with separate legislation. This is a business opportunity, which India should not miss! (Paldi, 2016)

As per International Association of Islamic Banks to ban interest and support PLS system is supported by economic rationales like:

a) The soundness of the project will decide the allocation of funds as per PLS system and the returns on capital is dependent on productivity. This will result in improvement of efficient capital allocation.

b) The PLS system ensures equitable distribution of wealth and will result in creation of wealth for its owners as compared to the system based on interest.

c) The system of interest free banking which has PLS system will increase the volume of investments resulting in creation of jobs, while the interest based system accepts those projects which have higher returns than the cost of debt.

d) Islamic finance limit speculation and trading in stocks and investment based on Profit sharing basis. This ensures liquidity to the shareholders.

e) In the PLS system if practiced in entirety ensures the supply of money not overstepping the supply of goods and thus reduce inflationary pressure in the economy.

With the decision by the current government Islamic banking has seen a first case in Maharashtra as mentioned in DNA India Report, 2016.

"In the most recent a first in the mainstream banking sector in Maharashtra, a cooperative bank controlled by BJP leader and state cooperation minister Subhash Deshmukh has launched Sharia-compliant Islamic banking. Here, interest-free deposits will be accepted from both Muslims and non-Muslims and distributed largely to the needy from the minority community at zero rates of interest to ensure their financial inclusion.

So far, the Lokmangal Cooperative Bank Ltd, controlled by Deshmukh, has distributed Rs 2.50 lakh to poor Muslims through the route. The minister will now call on other banks and financial institutions in Maharashtra to follow suit and adopt this model, which is also referred to as participatory banking." DNA, 2016.

4.4   Islamic Banking System-Potential in India

India maybe proved as a major market for Islamic Banking Institutions as it is having a large number of Muslim people. But this potential is contingent upon the favourable modifications and changes in the banking regulatory framework and increased awareness and financial literacy among Muslims and other people in India. Several studies have revealed that India has the prospective to emerge as a significantly large market for Islamic banking institutions and companies, provided there is a favourable change in regulatory framework and increased awareness among Muslims and others in India as a whole. One of the studies concluded that, given favourable regulatory conditions, India holds a promising growth opportunity for Islamic financial institutions, whose asset base globally is expected to more than triple to $1 trillion by 2016.

According to market experts and data analysis services provider Grail Research, Islamic banking system is rapidly gaining importance amongst the international monetary institutions, especially in the backdrop of the banking industry distresses affecting the markets such as the USA and UK and the idea of Islamic banking system has enormous prospective markets in India as well. According to Report by Grail Research, part of US-based management consultancy Monitor Group, India possibly will be a substantial market for Islamic financial institutions, as long as there is a constructive changes in regulatory framework and increased consciousness amongst Muslims and India. According to Grail Research Founder and CEO Mr Colin Gounden "You need to look no further than at the profitability of Saudi banks (the world's highest) for reasons why Islamic finance will have strong interest globally as a growth engine for financial services."

Al Rahmatullah, Professor, University of Calicut, concluded "The size of the market will be very large as the Indian population is above 100 crore and Muslim population itself is about 15 crore and majority of them, in the name of religious faith, are looking for interest free banking and finance."

India with a highest percentage of Muslim population in a non-Islamic country should have been in the front position of Islamic banking initiatives, but it is yet to be legalised here. It will enormously help the Indian economic system by drawing investments from the high net worth and cash rich Middle Eastern countries as well as other foreign countries on the lookout for new investment destinations.

Five Indian companies, Reliance Industries, Infosys Technologies Wipro, Tata Motors and Satyam Computer Services figure in the Standard & Poor's BRIC Shariah Index. The government of India has rejected the idea which advocates the introduction of Islamic Banking practices and its financial instruments in developing economies of Asia. But simultaneously it is worth to be noted that Indian government did not rule out the option of Islamic financial system for overseas branches and subsidiaries of Indian banks. Reserve Bank of India is bearing in mind various requirements for overseas branches and subsidiaries for offering Islamic Banking and financial services as well as financial instruments so that these institutions may capitalise the benefits of emerging markets.

4.4.1 Investments in Sharia Compliant Funds

Most of the investors do not invest in mutual funds or debt based funds as they perceive that it is forbidden, as per Islamic shariah (non halal) to invest in stock market interest related products. But there are various corporations which qualify for investment as per Islamic rules and one can invest in them through Shariah compliant funds. These funds will help one invest one's funds in shariah compliant companies and also decontaminate non-Shariah compliant income (non halal income).In long period equity investments may breed inflation thrashing returns. Shariah compliant investments refer to investments which comply with principals and rules of Islam. It is illegitimate hence forbidden as per Islamic Sharia to invest in the following.

- Alcohol
- Tobacco
- Gambling
- Pornography, drugs etc
- armaments and destructive weapons
- pork and related by-products;
- dead animals not slaughtered according to the rules of the Sharia(non halal food products) gold and silver armaments and destructive weapons
- Institutions like banks which generate income from interest payment.
- Companies with high debt.
- Any other activity which as per Shariah board violates Islamic religious principles.

They deploy services of premier third party Shariah advisory institutions to make sure Shariah compliance. Shariah board of such institutions screen and continuously checks the stocks for Shariah compliance. Stocks are regularly added and deleted based on their Shariah compliance status.

Shariah board also advises on identification and purification of non Shariah compliant incomes produced by Sharia compliant mutual funds. Non Shariah compliant returns are given as charity and/or donations.

4.4.2 Performance of Shariah Compliant Funds

In long term (5 years or more) the Shariah compliant funds have outperformed their counterparts. Thus one would not suffer losses by making investments in Shariah compliant fund. Even Non-Muslims who are willing to invest in ethical companies may think about these investment options.

List of Shariah Compliant firms

It is important to know about Sharia compliant funds as many companies have claimed to be Sharia compliant as there are very few alternatives left with people who avoid interest and want to earn some income by making investments in such stocks which will not clash with their faith and also ensure good returns. Thus Idafa Investment Pvt. Ltd. which is a Sharia compliant stocks investment firm had released a list of BSE 500 companies which were selected on the Sharia value system in the Investors' Education Programme organised by Idafa Investments Pvt. Ltd. in Mumbai. It was brought to knowledge about the selection of Sharia compliant stocks and the screening of such stocks which are involved in production or sales of liquor, tobacco, pornography, gambling, finance and banking industries and other financial conditions like:

(a) A company must not have interest based borrowings more than 33% of its market capitalisation.

(b) Interest earning should not be more than 5% of its total income

(c) Receivable (current + long term) should not be more than 45% of the total assets.

The list of such companies selected on Islamic parameters as mentioned above quantitatively and qualitatively as published in The Milli gazette as given in Table 4.5. There could have been more such companies now as the list was published in 2005 and there is a possibility that some of the companies might have got removed from the list thus it is important to make an investigation before making any investments in these companies.

Table 4.5 List of Shariah Compliant Funds

S.N.	Company Name	Economic Activity	Borrowings	Interest Earning	Receivables
1	Aban Loyd Chiles Offshore Ltd.	Yes	Yes	Yes	Yes
2	Abbott India Ltd.	Yes	Yes	Yes	Yes
3	Abhishek Industries Ltd.	Yes	Yes	Yes	Yes
4	Aftek Infosys Ltd.	Yes	Yes	Yes	Yes
5	Agro Tech Foods Ltd.	Yes	Yes	Yes	Yes
6	Alfa Laval (India) Ltd.	Yes	Yes	Yes	Yes
7	Ambuja Cement Eastern Ltd.	Yes	Yes	Yes	Yes
8	Amtek Auto Ltd.	Yes	Yes	Yes	Yes
9	Apollo Hospitals Enterprise Ltd.	Yes	Yes	Yes	Yes
10	Aptech Ltd.	Yes	Yes	Yes	Yes
11	Asahi India Glass Ltd.	Yes	Yes	Yes	Yes
12	Ashok Leyland Ltd.	Yes	Yes	Yes	Yes
13	Asian Paints (India) Ltd.	Yes	Yes	Yes	Yes
14	Associated Cement Cos. Ltd.	Yes	Yes	Yes	Yes
15	Astra Microwave Products Ltd.	Yes	Yes	Yes	Yes
16	Astrazeneca Pharma India Ltd.	Yes	Yes	Yes	Yes
17	Atlas Copco (India) Ltd.	Yes	Yes	Yes	Yes
18	Automotive Axles Ltd.	Yes	Yes	Yes	Yes
19	Aventis Pharma Ltd.	Yes	Yes	Yes	Yes
20	Aztec Software & Technology Services Ltd.	Yes	Yes	Yes	Yes
21	B O C India Ltd.	Yes	Yes	Yes	Yes
22	Bajaj Auto Ltd.	Yes	Yes	Yes	Yes
23	Bajaj Tempo Ltd.	Yes	Yes	Yes	Yes
24	Balmer Lawrie & Co. Ltd.	Yes	Yes	Yes	Yes
25	Bata India Ltd.	Yes	Yes	Yes	Yes
26	Berger Paints India Ltd.	Yes	Yes	Yes	Yes
27	Bharat Earth Movers Ltd.	Yes	Yes	Yes	Yes
28	Bharat Electronics Ltd.	Yes	Yes	Yes	Yes

29	Bharat Forge Ltd.	Yes	Yes	Yes	Yes
30	Bharat Petroleum Corpn. Ltd.	Yes	Yes	Yes	Yes
31	Bharati Shipyard Ltd.	Yes	Yes	Yes	Yes
32	Bilcare Ltd.	Yes	Yes	Yes	Yes
33	Biocon Ltd.	Yes	Yes	Yes	Yes
34	Birla Corporation Ltd.	Yes	Yes	Yes	Yes
35	Blue Dart Express Ltd.	Yes	Yes	Yes	Yes
32	Bilcare Ltd.	Yes	Yes	Yes	Yes
33	Biocon Ltd.	Yes	Yes	Yes	Yes
34	Birla Corporation Ltd.	Yes	Yes	Yes	Yes
35	Blue Dart Express Ltd.	Yes	Yes	Yes	Yes
36	Bombay Dyeing & Mfg. Co. Ltd.	Yes	Yes	Yes	Yes
37	Bongaigaon Refinery & Petrochemicals Ltd.	Yes	Yes	Yes	Yes
38	Britannia Industries Ltd.	Yes	Yes	Yes	Yes
39	Cadila Healthcare Ltd.	Yes	Yes	Yes	Yes
40	Castrol India Ltd.	Yes	Yes	Yes	Yes
41	Century Enka Ltd.	Yes	Yes	Yes	Yes
42	Ciba Specialty Chemicals (India) Ltd.	Yes	Yes	Yes	Yes
43	Cipla Ltd.	Yes	Yes	Yes	Yes
44	Clariant (India) Ltd.	Yes	Yes	Yes	Yes
45	Colgate-Palmolive (India) Ltd.	Yes	Yes	Yes	Yes
46	Container Corpn. Of India Ltd.	Yes	Yes	Yes	Yes

Source: Compiled by Author from The Milli Gazette, June,4, 2005

4.5 Feasibility of Islamic Banking

There are a lot of pre conceived notions about the feasibility of Islamic banking. Here such notions are discussed and how to come forward from these notions are also discussed to understand the feasibility of an interest free bank in an interest based economy.

a) As Islamic banks have a commitment in share of losses there will be people who will be dealing with the banks on PLS basis will incur huge losses which will lead to failure and bankruptcy.

b) Islamic banks may experience more defaults and will conceal their real earnings which will affect the stability of Islamic banks.

c) It will be a tough situation for Islamic banks to perform all its financial activities without interest in an environment which is interest based.

Now to break this preconceived notion it is important to understand certain issues and nuances of Islamic banking functions like

i) Some Muslim authors have put forward the argument that since Islamic banks have to share losses this does not mean that it will lead to its failure as Islamic banks operate on the basis of a diversified portfolio so that even if there are individual cases of losses can be maintained by pooling of risks.

ii) As per defaults are concerned there are three main reasons for the possibility of defaults the nature of the client to whom finance is provided, the purpose for finance and the type of supervision by the banks for the use of the funds. These factors are to be taken care in terms of loans irrespective of whether the bank is commercial bank or Islamic bank. In fact as Islamic bank is having a direct stake in the profit and loss of the business it is more vigilant in the end use of funds as compared to commercial bank which is more interested in earning of the interest component in the instalments of the loans.

iii) Concealment of exact profits due to non payment of share in profits cannot be the basis of instability of Islamic banks. As over the period of time incentive to cheat will get reduced as loss of reputation will affect future credit access. Some measures taken by Islamic banks can counter such misgivings like:

iv) Cheating by under reporting of profits can be challenged in court in a Mudaraba contract.

v) Defaulters or cheaters can be blacklisted and denied any further funds from the entire banking system will act as a deterrent for such unlawful practices.

vi) The misgiving as mentioned that Islamic banks will have to face a tough time working in an interest based system though it can make some provisions to stay away with interest and still work with commercial banks like maintaining a current account with the commercial corresponding bank, to correct a debit balance in their account with corresponding bank and it has to be ensured by the corresponding bank to not to charge any interest on the temporary debit balance of the Islamic bank as it is also not obliged to pay any compensation for their credit balances.

4.6 Risks Associated with Islamic Banks and Measures for Mitigation

Commercial banks make use of both debt and equity to finance their investments, while Islamic banks have to primarily depend upon equity financing and customers' deposit accounts such as current, saving, and investment (Karim and Ali, 1989).

Grais and Kulathunga (2007) have summarized with their research the main risks that any bank might face are under four broad categories:

1-Financial risk:

a- Credit risk: It is the risk of the counterparty failure to meet their obligation towards the bank in a timely manner.

b- Interest rate risk: It is the risk of the reduction in the value of the fixed-interest asset such as bonds due to a rise in interest rates. This can be also considered as part of market risk, unless the asset is in the banking book. Also, interest rate risk is the risk of an interest rate mismatch between fixed-rate assets and floating-rate liabilities, or vice-versa, which results in a "squeeze" in both profit and cash flow.

c- Market risk: It is a risk which affects the class of assets or liabilities to a bank due to economic changes or external events. It is also considered as a systematic risk such as changes in stock market, interest rates, currency or commodity markets.

d- Liquidity risk: It is either a financing liquidity risk which arises from the difficulty of obtaining funding at a reasonable cost or an asset liquidity risk which arises from the difficulty of trading an asset.

e- Settlement risk: The risk that counterparty does not deliver security or their values in cash as per agreement when the security is traded after other counterparty have delivered security or cash as per agreement.

f- Prepayment risk: The risk of loans being prepaid before maturity date, especially when it comes to mortgage loans. This can take place due to a drop in interest rates.

2-Operational risk: are risks which mainly result from inadequate internal processes and strategies, people and systems, or from external events. This is associated with the potential for systems failure in a given market.

3-Business risk:

a- Legal and Regulatory risk: The type of risk that arise due to the changes in the law and regulations which adversely affect a bank's position.

- b- Volatility risk: This is the risk which arises from the fluctuations in the exchange rate of currencies.
- c- Equity risk: This risk is mainly due to stock market dynamics which lead to depreciation of investments.
- d- Country risk: A political or financial event in a particular country might lead to potential volatility of those foreign assets.

4-Event risk: Unpredictable risks due to unforeseen events such as banking crisis.

Siddiqui (2008) concluded that Islamic banks have to face similar risk as faced by commercial banks, though there are certain differences as Islamic banks have to abide by

1. Commodities and Inventory risk: This type of risk arises from holding items in inventory either for resale under a Murabaha contract or for leasing under Ijara. For information, the collateral under Islamic banking is established at the time of financing and the borrower becomes the owner of the assets to be purchased through financing and if default occurs, the bank can confiscate those collateral assets, which it owns for the tenor of the contract.

2. Rate of return risk: This type of risk is similar to the interest rate risk in the banking book, even though Islamic banks are not exposed to interest rate risks. They are only exposed to a "squeeze" resulting from holding a fixed-return asset such as the Murabaha that are financed by investment accounts in the liabilities.

3. Legal and Sharia compliance risk: There are operational risks in failing to ensure Sharia compliance and risks associated with the potential of systems failure resulting from inadequate internal processes and strategies, people, and external events. As a result, this includes legal and Sharia Compliance risk.

4. Equity position risk in banking book: This arises from the equity exposure in Mudaraba and Musharakah financing contracts.
5. Mark-up risk (benchmark risk): As Islamic banks do not use interest, they use market rates as benchmarks in pricing their financing contracts and products. As a result, the risk will arise from any change that will happen to the benchmark rates used, and are also interrelated to the risk of rate of return that is mentioned earlier.

In a study by Khan and Ahmed (2001) 17 Islamic financial institutions from 10 countries have ranked the risk faced by the institutions. The results reveal that credit risk is faced both by Islamic and conventional banks but the Islamic banks have to face another critical risk that is mark up risk, followed by operational risk and liquidity risk, credit risk and market risk.

The tools for mitigation of these risks are usually not based on Sharia which is a constraint for Islamic banks.

Thus the Basel Committee has predetermined a higher minimum capital requirement for Islamic Banks. Also as the Islamic banks are using a PLS model for financing in which the principal amount is not guaranteed in certain contracts thus there should be a higher capital adequacy requirement (Errico and Farahbaksh, 1998). This will ensure a better solvency and investors' protection. Ainley (2000) supporting the same view that Islamic banks deal in new and unfamiliar forms of finance where assets are long-term Ainley (2000) articulated that Islamic banks transact in new and different structure of finance where assets are long-term and illiquid. Thus, regulators should impose higher capital requirements on Islamic banks, particularly during the early years of an Islamic bank operation.

4.7   Islamic Banking Worldwide

These days there is a trend amongst organizations to be more socially responsible, and take initiatives in the welfare of the society, and it is no wonder that Islamic banking has also found a place in identifying with this concept. Interest is the core part of the banking business but as mentioned earlier also as per the views of some philosophers it has led to disparities also in the system. With this interest based traditional environment it is interesting that Islamic banks are working and growing with the ideology of no interest in terms of its asset base, capital and consumers. There are over 280 Islamic banks operating in 50 countries with the asset base of $250 million to $300 billion from Jakarta to Jeddah.

There are several foreign banks operating in India like Standard Chartered Bank, Citibank, HSBC have interest free windows in West Asian countries, Europe and the USA. Several discussions and committees have expressed the need of Islamic banks in India, though without proper regulation it will be difficult to adopt such a system by the present commercial banks.

Interest free banks have been misjudged as a religious venture restricted to a particular community and its successful operations and growth around the world has been neglected.

Islamic banks have the same purpose as that of commercial banks except for the fact that Islamic banks work on the principles of Sharia (Islamic Law). It is infact a package of services like Islamic bonds (sukuk), Islamic insurance (takaful), credit cards, online banking, ATMs and other state of the art services which have a huge potential in India.

As per the Dow Jones Islamic Index 60-70% of Indian companies on the BSE and NSE as Sharia compliant for equity investment. And there are around 200 small Islamic Institutions in the state of Kerala. In western countries major banks have opened special no interest divisions to cater to their customers who are avoiding interest.

Though the need has been identified but it is a niche market of clients with special needs and there is a long road ahead for the spread of Islamic banking and more research and policy making have to be done by policy makers and the major players in the banking sector who can bring upon the change to cater to the special needs of the niche section of the society willing to forgo interest for the reasons of faith.

4.8 Benefits from Islamic Banking

Islamic Banking if introduced in India can prove to be beneficial to the Muslim community and to the country in various ways:

a) Economic growth with financial inclusion- As mentioned in the earlier chapter also that financial inclusion is a problem which has to be tackled by the government. As per Sachar Committee Report also the socio economic status of Muslim community is very poor. Thus Muslims who have inhibition in banking with interest based banks can come up and bank with the interest free banks without hurting their religious sentiments. There would also be more opportunities for people who can have finance available to them not on the basis of interest but equity.

b) Growth in FDI: With the introduction of Interest free banking Muslims will get an acceptable mode of finance and investment, which will motivate retail investors as well as encourage foreign direct investment (FDI) from participating and making investments in India especially from the renowned businesses from Gulf Countries.

c) Availability of Funds for Business: With Islamic banking coming in India there will be an assurance of availability of funds for business required for tools, machinery and equipment under the scheme of Ijara which is actually lease and purchase. Also Murabahah that is cost plus financing can help businessmen in financing the raw material required for starting up their business. Thus Islamic banking will help in establishing and starting up small businesses to big businesses.

d) Free from Exploitation: Dr Mohammad Umar Chapra Renowned scholar and senior consultant to the Islamic Research Institute of the Islamic Development Bank, Saudi Arabia, has emphasized the requirement to implement Islamic Banking and economy system to set up a true welfare state. Dr Chapra views that with the adoption of Islamic banking in the economy, such a society can be made where people would be free from exploitation and basic needs of people are met.

4.9 Demonetisation and Interest Avoiding Population

It has been observed that since the demonetisation has taken place people who did not have any bank account are coming up to deposit cash. In an excerpt from Times of India it was mentioned that "Under Shariah law, any transaction that involves interest, or Riba, is considered illegal. Therefore, Noman's grandmother, and many others like her, never had a bank account. People view the modern banking system with much suspicion because of religious reasons. And some people opened account just to deposit their money which they had stored and not invested in any venture, nor bothered to open an account with the bank. That's a positive thing. Prof Jawed Ahmed Khan of Jamia's Centre for Western Studies said the move would compel Muslims to come out and put money in bank accounts. This will have a positive impact on the society and they could use banks, but only if they have the option of Islamic banking, Khan said." (Times of India, 2016) it can be stated that Muslims have been doubtful in the practice of commercial banking as it clashes with the faith of a Muslim, with the current situation due to demonetisation they might come and deposit their stored cash in the bank and might open a new account but it does not guarantee their adherence to the commercial banking system. For letting them stay in the banking system it is important for the government to make efforts in bringing the interest free banking system.

For the possibilities of interest free banking in India there is a need to discuss the financial system from legal and other angles which is the subject matter of the next chapter.

CHAPTER-5

CHALLENGES FOR ISLAMIC BANKING IN INDIA: EXPECTED FRAMEWORK

The present chapter is devoted to the discussion on the expected framework for Islamic banking in India with especial reference to the principles of Islamic banking, role of Islamic banking, performance of Islamic banking during recent global financial crises and the challenges faced by Islamic baking in India.

5.1 Principles of Islamic Banking for India

Before going through the regulatory framework of Islamic Banking in India it is important to known the solutions which can come if Islamic banking comes into existence, due to which other countries have adopted Islamic banking and are exploring the possibilities of the same. Financial inclusion is one of the goals of the government but how far it has been successful to achieve the same. Here such issues are discussed and solutions to these issues are being sought in Islamic banking.

Today it is seen that every industry has to work not only for earning money but also be socially responsible in the society in which it exists. Corporate social responsibility is seen as a major work done by industries and every industry has to make contribution to the society from where they are earning money. Thus banking industry also has to act responsibly towards the society.

Islamic finance does not only aim in improving the materialistic issues of economy but also aims to achieve human welfare and well being with an emphasis on socio economic justice, community values and by striking a correct balance between spiritual and material needs of its followers. The main principles on which Islamic banking is based upon can be applied to India as:

- Interest prohibition: As per Islam interest is prohibited either in the form of earning or giving thus a financial transaction should be free from interest (Riba) and directly or indirectly should be linked to a real economic transaction. Seeking profit from someone's indebtedness or trading in debts is unethical. The debtor and creditor should share the risks and profits generated from the project. The prohibition of interest is the basic principle of the Islamic economy based on the principle of social justice, rights and equity. Interest on the other hand rewards to those who have not made any effort in the project nor do they have any participation except for the financing of the project. Money earning money is not a valid concept in Islam and thus it violates the concept of social justice. Islam is not against earning of money but it prohibits earning money at the cost of others by socially oppressing others. Thus, to create an environment free from exploitation and oppression an economic environment needs to be adopted based on fairness and social justice. As it is fairer that the provider of the finance is also concerned with the fate of the project and not just reclining on the fixed return from the repayment of loan. The financer should also be involved from the start to end of the project, the risks faced by the entrepreneur that is how a system of harmony can be seen even between a creditor and debtor in the economy.
- No dealing in unlawful assets: there should be any dealing with investments being made in unlawful sectors like businesses dealing in alcohol, drugs, tobacco, harmful substances, gambling, tobacco, pork, etc. These things are forbidden in Islam thus any association in these kinds of activities which is considered 'haram' that is prohibited, for businesses would mean getting involved in these activities which is forbidden or prohibited. These kinds of

businesses are also harmful for the society, many families are in distress due to these things in the society and as Islam aims in eradicating such problems from the society from the root level thus such a system has to be made where these things cannot be accessed and thus a better society can be formed.

- There is also a prohibition on transactions which involve any kind of speculation or gambling known as Maiser, and also on uncertainty or ambiguity in transactions known as gharar, any transactions in which terms and conditions are not clear will come in this category. Black marketing and hoarding will also come in this category as this will unnecessary push the prices and will be harmful to the society at large, that is why these kinds of transactions which increases the risk of speculation at the cost of society is prohibited.

Thus it can be said that Islamic business principles are based on fair trading policies, human welfare, and well being of society, fair and clear dealings. All the transactions are based on tangible and identifiable underlying asset. (Ben Arab, 2009).

5.2 Financial Inclusion through Islamic Banking

The innate social justice prospective of Islamic economics is an underutilized resource for poverty eradication. Presently, Islamic microfinance is phased in such a manner to grow the market of Islamic banking and finance by navigating the poor population into formal financial activities. By expansion of the reach of Islamic microfinance through funding strategies can help in meeting the needs of the poor. In this regard, Islamic finance has tremendous potential from zakat, waqf and sadaqat to streamline it and channel it towards various financial goals.

The value of worldwide Islamic financial assets is growing quickly; since the 1970s, assets have leapt from half a million dollars to more than two trillion USD. This number is expected to increase to 3.4 trillion USD by 2018.

The IBF industry has long been dominated by advanced economies in the Persian Gulf, but now the fastest-growing markets are more spread across the world. The slow-but-steady growth of Islamic microfinance has recently become dynamic – fuelled by increased attention from governments, central banks, donors, and IBF institutions.

As noted in the report: "Islamic (Micro) Finance: Culture, Context, Promise and Challenges", for better understanding Islamic microfinance and the role it is playing, cultural contexts should be examined as well to get an account for knowing the factors. With the experience of the clients as mentioned in the report through structured interviews and participant observation the more complex financial tools can be understood with the customers' perspective.

This addresses methodological challenges in microfinance research: banks, acting as gatekeepers, can (un) intentionally restrict access for researchers. The need for the poor to ensure continued access to banks can affect their responses to market research and customer surveys.

The report highlights the historical background of the financial products, summarizes the in depth examination of Islamic microfinance in countries like Bangladesh, Pakistan and Indonesia. Challenges faced by female clients in female headed households, client relationship with officers, accounting challenges. The report also suggests for the digitisation of services to meet the needs of the poor and to eradicate certain inefficiencies in the system.

The capacity for innovation in this still-nascent industry, where supply has not met demand, should encourage impatient optimism of industry observers, providers, and clients alike. (Kustin, 2015)

5.2.1 Financial Inclusion

Financial inclusion means to make financial services available to every strata of the society as against the financial exclusion which is available for particular strata of the society.

The term "financial inclusion" has become famous since early 2000s, by finding a direct relationship between poverty and financial exclusion. The United Nations have defined financial inclusion "as providing access at a reasonable cost for all households to a full range of financial services, including savings or deposit services, payment and transfer services, credit and insurance, sound and safe institutions governed by clear regulation and industry performance standards, financial and institutional sustainability, to ensure continuity and certainty of investment, and competition to ensure choice and affordability for clients"

(AusAID, 2010)

5.2.2 Financial Inclusion Index

CRISIL, India's credit rating agency had launched an index on June 25, 2013 for measuring the status of financial inclusion in India. The index called as Inclusix is a kind of tool to measure the financial inclusion in India, in 632 districts. It is a relative index on a scale of 0 to 100, and it combines the three parameters of banking services which are branch penetration, deposit penetration and credit penetration as one metric.

The report has highlighted the first regional state wise, district wise assessments of financial inclusion in a three year time period. Some key findings from the report are as follows:

a) The CRISIL Inclusix score in 2013 is of 40.1 which is low, and this score has improved from 35.4 in 2009.
b) The major factor of financial inclusion is deposit penetration and the number of savings accounts which is 624 million is almost four times to the number of loan accounts that is 160 million.
c) During 2009-11, 618 districts out of 632 reported improvement in their scores.
d) The top three states and Union Territories are Puducherry, Chandigarh, and Kerala; the top three districts are Pathanamthitta (Kerala), Karaikal (Puducherry), and Thiruvananthapuram (Kerala).(CRISIL,2013)
e) Microfinance which worked as a tool for financial inclusion was used aggressively by the microfinance institutions and had a very sad state in Andhra Pradesh which had one third of microfinance industry of India. These institutions were blamed to exploit the poor farmers as they defaulted on the loans which led to farmers' suicide and this led to the politicisation of the entire situation which led to the collapse of the microfinance industry.

"India's rapidly growing private microcredit industry faces imminent collapse as almost all borrowers in one of India's largest states have stopped repaying their loans, egged on by politicians who accuse the industry of earning outsize profits on the backs of the poor."(New York Times, 2010)

There have been various discussions in different parts of the world to include every person and give financial facilities to the individual and to create awareness of the financial services by the banking sector and financial institutions for the upliftment of the society and this can be achieved if every individual is able to use these services. So now the question arises how Islamic banking can help in this matter?

There are certain individuals who in spite of being aware of the banking facilities around them and who are capable of opening a bank account and other banking services are not doing so due to religious reasons.

For instance, the religious scriptures like The Torah and Talmud have encouraged granting of loans without interest having certain exceptions like charging of interest is considered as among the worst sins according to the Book of Ezekiel and is forbidden as per the Jewish law.

Going by the references from the religious scriptures like Exodus 22:25–27, Leviticus 25:36–37 and Deuteronomy 23:20–21. In Leviticus loans are encouraged, whether of money or food, but also emphasize that they facilitate the poor to resume their independence, like in the other two places in the Bible, forbids the charging of interest on the loan.

In the Quran there are twelve verses which states prohibition of interest, citing a few verses from the Quran also shows the prohibition of interest 3:130 "O you who have believed, do not consume usury, doubled and multiplied, but fear Allah that you may be successful."

2:275 "Allah has permitted trade and has forbidden interest."

Thus there are certain individuals who give preference to interest free banking as compared to conventional banking even if the former is expensive. In a study conducted researchers have found that in the sample, there is an evidence of a imaginary preference for Sharia-compliant products among a number of respondents despite higher costs. However, 37 percent of respondents report that they would prefer a cheaper conventional loan or that they have no preference.(Kunt,Klapper,Randall, 2013)

Mahmoud Mohieldin who had been the managing director of the World Bank wrote that Islamic finance "has the potential to meet more people's banking and investment needs, expand its reach, and contribute to greater financial stability and inclusion in the developing world" (Mohieldin, 2012).

Talking about financial inclusion and Muslims it is important to study about Sachar Committee report of 2006 which has proven that Muslims in India are more financially excluded than the rest of the population; the real reason could be that Muslims have an aversion for interest based products and services which are against their faith. This was pointed out by the former RBI Governor Raghuram Rajan in 2008.

As per the study by (Honohon, 2007) about 72% Muslims living in Muslim majority countries are not using financial services, as they view the commercial banking products and services clashing with the principles of their faith. In recent years there have been attempts to cater to low income Muslim clients some MFIs have customised their services in a way through which they can provide financial services to such Muslim clients. It is a practice of combining micro finance with Islamic banking which, is a new trend catching up in the world as highlighted by Karim Nimrah et.al 2008.

These studies show that there are people in the society who prefer interest free banking even if they incur additional charges to get the service as they are looking for a solution to their financial services which will satiate their spiritual desires too.

By going back to the Microfinance debacle in India it is quite evident that poor people just do not need loans they want a complete solution to their problems, issues, technical knowhow to help them establish their businesses and work out a solution for them.

With the conventional microfinance system which was applied in Andhra Pradesh their problems multiplied as before they could even start their business they had to pay their EMIs which had the component of interest in it. So if they have taken a loan of Rs.20000 to meet their ends and paying an interest of 10% for 12 months they are paying Rs.2196 more on their loan. This was an example just to explain the situation although the loans had much more interest than this and that too compounded annually and that too for a more period of time.

In the article "In partial agreement with SKS on what caused the Indian Microfinance Crash" Mader Philip has pointed about some Indian politicians who had begun to spot the thought of eradicating poverty with microfinance as useless.

Fig. 5.1 M- CRIL Growth Index

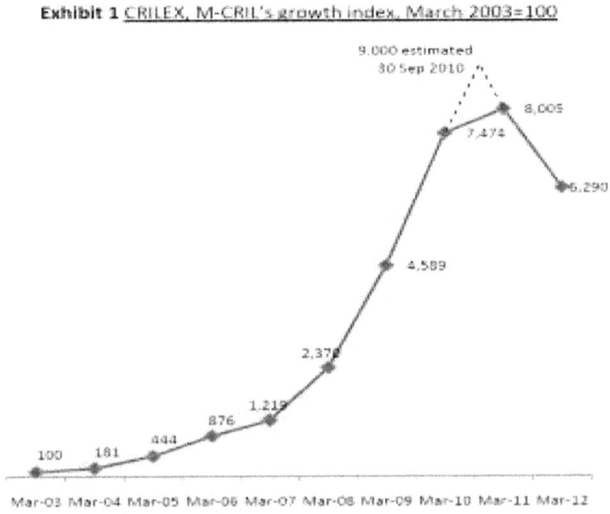

Exhibit 1 CRILEX, M-CRIL's growth index, March 2003=100

Source: M-CRIL Microfinance Review 2012 (vii)

In India the microfinance industry has seen a decline since 2010 as can be seen from the (Fig.5.1). The performance of microfinance industry is deteriorating and the blame game is going on for the wrongdoings happened in Andhra Pradesh and industry has blamed the government's legislation responsible for the dozens of suicides due to non payment of loans.

(Mader Philip, 2013)

5.2.3 Islamic Banking under Recession Period

The results show that Islamic banks may be more shielded to economic crises which may be due to the fact that they do not take on as much risk. Most Interest free banks are quite small in terms of their total assets compared to commercial banks. It would be interesting to further investigate the question of the size of a bank's effect on its change in profit with a larger sample of banks that includes Islamic and conventional banks. The prominence of larger Islamic banks may have the potential to strengthen a country's financial system and help mitigate a recession's impact on the financial services industry as a whole. (Muhammad Ismail Memon, 2013)

An IMF study had compared the performance of Islamic banks and commercial banks during the recent financial crisis, and found that Islamic banks, on average, showed stronger resistance during the global financial crisis. (IMF Survey Online, 2010). The introduction of Islamic banking in India will strengthen the Indian financial system even in recessionary period as evident from the performance of Islamic banks during the recent global financial crises.

5.3 Islamic Banking: Lessons from other Countries

Ernst and Young (E&Y) the business consulting firm in its World Islamic Banking Competitiveness Report had shown the assets of Interest free banks grew at 17% per year from the year 2008 to 2012. This rate is two to three times faster than the growth of commercial banks in the same period. It could be as there is a difference in functioning of Sharia compliant banks and commercial banks and the economic growth is stronger in the upcoming markets of the countries with a huge Muslim population.

E&Y had identified 25 "rapid growth market" nations which they have predicted will be accounting for half of the global GDP by 2020. Out of these, 10 countries have a high Muslim population. Iran had accounted for half of the banking assets in Islamic banks worldwide.

The QISMUT nations namely, (Qatar, Indonesia, Saudi Arabia, Malaysia, UAE and Turkey) where average growth had been 6.5% for the past five years, have three fourth of the Islamic banking assets. The reason for rapid expansion of Islamic banking is mainly through Islamic windows in conventional banks rather than in pure Islamic banks. With this existing banks can get into Islamic banking market conveniently.

As per E & Y's estimate there is a scope for 20% growth for every year in the next five years. As even in countries where Islamic banking is there like the Gulf state and in South East Asia its share accounts for more than one third of the market. In Indonesia which has the world's most Muslim population Islamic banking has less than 5% of market share.

There are other nations too in which there is a huge Muslim population which is untapped by Islamic banking like Pakistan, India, Bangladesh, Nigeria, Morocco, Egypt and a number of other countries in former Soviet Republic. The UK also had shown intent by issuing £200 million sukuk or Islamic bond. The British government with an aim of making London as a centre for Islamic finance in the West has entered the Islamic banking sector.

(Yueh, BBC News, 2014)

Islamic finance has a deep connection with real economy, which offers ethical investments and financing options for enterprises. The tenets of Islamic finance encourage inclusion and mutual co-operation for the creation of a fair and equitable financial system that everyone has access to. In the past 30 years Islamic finance has achieved exceptional growth and is being supported by Muslims and Non Muslims. It has made its presence to most nations of the world. But still, there is much potential for Islamic banking in achieving further growth.

Though Islamic banking is based on the social welfare of the society but its development will not be complete if more such initiatives are taken to address the problems of the society. In regard to this, charity needs to prioritise as a key area of business. With the introduction of banking products and services specially designed for charity it would be a novel way of facilitating donations to societies' marginalised group.

Sadly, the major problem of poverty can be seen in many Muslim majority nations, and nearly half a billion of the world's poor who earn below $2 in a day, come from Indonesia, Pakistan, Egypt, Nigeria, Bangladesh. These people have tried hard to meet their ends and such people are needy and Islamic banking should take initiatives to reach out to these nations and support them to eradicate poverty and try to give them a decent sustenance.

(Vilarino, Devex News, 2015)

5.4 Challenges for Islamic Banking in India

There are going to be challenges for Islamic banking in India and it cannot come automatically there have to be amendments in the laws and regulations of the banking industry for welcoming Islamic Banking in India in fact that is a major hurdle for existence of Islamic banking in India. Some of the challenges which can be listed are:

1. Legal Issues: The laws of Indian banking system does not directly prohibit Islamic banking but there are certain provisions which make it an unviable option.
2. Certain provisions regarding this are mentioned below:
   - "Section 5 (b) and 5 (c) of the Banking Regulation Act, 1949 prohibit the banks to invest on Profit Loss Sharing basis -the very basis of Islamic banking."
   - Section 8 of the Banking Regulations Act (BR Act, 1949) states, "No banking company shall directly or indirectly deal in buying or selling or bartering of goods…"
   - "Section 9 of the Banking Regulations Act prohibits bank to use any sort of immovable property apart from private use –this is against Ijarah for home finance"
   - "Section 21 of the Banking Regulations Act requires payment of Interest which is against Sharia."
3. There was a time when the CRR and SLR had amounted to more than 50% of banks' deposits. Though now they have been reduced to a great extent but this does not ensure establishment of an Interest free bank.

4. Other obstacles in the way of Islamic banking are discussed below, the frequent changes, though for genuine reasons, in the regulatory framework of Indian financial sector become an important obstacle while some of these changes were in favor of Islamic financial institutions; a majority of them hindered their advancement. Earlier NBFCs were governed by Companies Act 1956, which did not even contain the definition of a finance company. The registration of these companies with RBI was made compulsory during April 1993 to March 1995.

5. The RBI amendment Act 1997 which had given a range of powers on RBI for the control of functioning of NBFCs. The latest amendments to NBFCs guidelines state that "An NBFC having certificate of registration and otherwise entitled to accept public deposits is allowed to open its branch/office or allow its agents to operate for enlistment of public deposits within the state where its registered office is situated if its NOF (not owned fund) is up to Rs. 50 crores and anywhere in India if its NOF is more than Rs. 50 crore and its fixed deposits program have been rated by one of the approved credit rating agencies at 'AA' or above". These amendments clip the wings of all Islamic financial companies (and they are already few) as none of them qualifies to operate beyond the state of its registered office.

6. An additional dilemma comes because of asymmetrical treatment of debt and equity fund. The capital of Islamic financial companies is equity-based operating through profit and loss sharing. Under the existing government rules profit is taxed while interest is exempted from tax on the ground that it is a cost item. This puts the Islamic financial institutions in the underprivileged position. Currently the rate of tax on dividend is 15%.

7. The precision in distribution of profits, appropriate records, maintenance of balance sheet, qualified personnel, financial skill, standard accounting procedure, compliance to existing government rules, with the Sharia principles are important fundamentals to support and refurbish investors' confidence. Sadly, on all these criteria, Islamic financial institutions in India have shown a plain disappointment.
8. Islam encourages the view of giving time to poor till he is able to his debt. But there is no clear guideline for intentional and rich defaulters. In the opinion of some scholars the rich defaulters should be fined to an extent and the amount thereof should be spent in charity. Though, this view needs to be comprehended upon to reach consensus.

There are some political opposition parties who have said "they will oppose introduction of Islamic banks. Because of the strict adherence to not paying or taking interest, Sharia banking will call for a complete overhaul of the banking regulatory system". There is also a concern that India does not have satisfactory manpower trained in interest free banking.

Khan (2010) in the article "Islamic Banks and Regulatory Framework in India" has thrown light on the challenges faced by Islamic banks in India and the possible conditions in which it can come to India. Khan (2010) mentioned that Islamic banks have not been set up in India due to regulatory compliances which are not compatible with Islamic Shariah which cannot be observed by these Islamic Institutions. Consequently, there have been numerous efforts to practice Islamic banking services through Non Banking Financial Companies (NBFCs), Cooperative Societies, Nidhies Islamic Funds etc. The initial capital for a new bank should be Rs 300 crores of which 40 per cent should be contributed by the promoters. The 60 percent should be raised through public issue or private placement. Promoters will have lock-in period of 5 years. The NRI participation can be up to 40 percent. Industrial houses can hold only up to 10 percent. It would be a Herculean task for us to mobilize Rs. 300 crores as initial capital. It may be highlighted that raising the capital through public issues require stringent disclosure norms and strong financial net worth. As regards NBFCs we need to meet the following conditions:

- Paid-up Capital = 2 Crores
- Credit Rating = AAA
- Capital Adequacy Ratio = 12 to 15 per cent and
- NPA = 5 per cent

1) Besides, if Islamic banks have to accept deposits, borrowed funds, funds through bonds, they have to participate in interest based banking.

2) Banks have to maintain cash with Reserve Bank of India which attract interest from RBI. Interest payment has been stopped by the R.B.I. on temporary basis

3) Banks have to invest 29 percent of demand and time liability in instruments for SLR. These instruments are unencumbered securities like government securities, bonds issued by NABARD,. IFCI, SIDBI, NHB, Government approved securities which are interest based.

4) Since Islamic banks cannot observe conditions as mentioned above they cannot be member of clearing system and cannot issue cheques and therefore they cannot be listed as scheduled bank.

5) Since Islamic bank will have to maintain 9 percent Capital Adequacy Ratio, they will have to get it through equity capital as well as through bonds for 2nd tier capital which goes partly against Shariah.

6) Islamic banks will have to diversify PS based investment instruments. As far as equity shares are concerned banks can invest only up to 5 percent of their demand and time deposits in this instrument.

7) Priority sector finance on micro level cannot be extended to 200 Million borrowers based on Profit Sharing. But this is mandatory requirement and it is interest based.

8) Since Islamic banks cannot be recognized as scheduled bank, RBI cannot play the role of lender of last resort to them.

9) Islamic banks cannot enter the money market.

10) Section 8 of banking companies specify that" no banking company shall directly or in-directly deal in buying or selling or bartering of goods except in connection with the security given to or held by it or engage in any trade or buy or sell or barter goods for others otherwise then in connection with bills of exchange received for collection".

11) A bank is also prohibited from engaging in buying or selling activities on behalf of others unless such activities are taken in connection of bills of exchange lodged with banks for collection so Istisna financing cannot be permitted for banks.

12) It would be seen from above that there is legal restriction and murabaha cannot be used in India. Indian banks however, can use mudarabah or musharaka in a limited way as banks can invest only up to 5 percent of their demand and time liabilities in equity shares but this cannot be a strategic finance.

13) Again banks cannot become the partner in business on musharakah basis. Indian banks cannot do hire purchase financing.

14) As regards lease financing, Act provides financing of purchase of goods which can be given on lease by the borrowers but the bank cannot be the partner as an owner in leasing activities because it is a commercial activity. However, an Islamic financial institution engaged in lease activity owns the equipment or capital throughout the life of asset and earns rental whereas according to Indian Act, the bank earns only interest on lease financing.

Under the Act (Banking Companies Act 1949) commercial banks are only allowed to trade except within their specified limit. The similar rule cannot be applied to Islamic banks which can establish trading company as a subsidiary to finance the credit purchase and as well as assets. These firms can buy commodities and assets and sell them back to their customers on the basis of deferred payment. This involves equity participation. However, Banking Act Section (19), sub-section (1) does allow a bank to open subsidiaries to do equity portfolio management, insurance services, housing finance, venture capital funds etc. These are wholly owned by the banks.

5.5 Risk Management

Reserve bank of India has introduced prudential norms management of operational risk, credit risk, internal rating system, capital adequacy assessments. Under the Basel committee risk management, financial stability and protection of interest of depositor is prime goal of regulations. In Islamic banking which is profit sharing financing, protection of deposits or capital is not guaranteed. Thus, there is a clash amid Islamic bank and banking regulation to protect the deposits of depositors.

Some major constraints for Islamic banking in the Indian Banking system in general are highlighted by Khan (2010) are:

- Cannot function as banks: As there is a condition of CRR and SLR in the country interest free banks cannot function as banks. As in maintaining the

CRR they have to maintain a deposit account with the RBI on which they get interest which is against the tenet of Islamic banking.

- Interest Based financial products and services: As Islamic banks should have no fraction of interest but if it has to function in India, it has to work under the license provided by the RBI. Consequently, the RBI cannot act as a lender of the last resort too because such a lending will also be interest based.

- Inability to Maintain Capital Adequacy: There would be a constraint for Islamic banking in maintenance of the adequate capital and would be unable to interact with interest based banks.

- Inability of evaluation of projects: Islamic banks will have to confine themselves to small and medium projects as for the long term projects it has to assess for its profitability and feasibility for which the technical assistance is required and Islamic banks due to their small operations cannot perform it.

- Legal Framework : As mentioned earlier too The banking regulation Act has certain provisions which cannot allow Islamic bank to function and with the current commercial bank only a service of a current account can be said interest free rest of the services need modification to be made interest free for which amendments have to be made.

- Tax Procedures: As there is a difference in the procedure of tax in respect to interest and profit so this difference will hinder the calculation of taxes in the Islamic banking system, as the tax system in India treats interest as a cost and profit as an income. Thus, this needs to be resolved for Islamic banking if it enters into the Indian system.

- Critics' view: Some Muslim critics of Islamic banking are of the view that Islamic banks have given a different nomenclature to the interest and they hide it with other names as done by European bankers in the middle ages, to allow the charging of interest as it was against the Church teachings.

5.6 Expected Framework for Islamic Banking in India

Raghuram Rajan former RBI Governor had, without naming Islamic banking, suggested the need to have an interest-free banking in India. "The non-availability of interest-free banking products (where the return to the investor is tied to the bearing of risk, in accordance with the principles of that faith) results in some Indians, including those in the economically disadvantaged strata of society, not being able to access banking products and services due to reasons of faith. This non-availability also denies India's access to substantial sources of savings from other countries in the region," the report said.

Another factor which stimulated the committee to take in proposition on Islamic banking was the Sachar committee report, "outlined the Muslim community being a victim of financial exclusion. The committee has recommended that micro-equity financing as a product should be included in mainstream banking. All banks and microfinance institutions should offer these micro-equity financing products."The Raghuram Rajan report, "while advocating the introduction of Islamic banking in India, has made a commendable contribution in the cause of Islamic banking by justifying it with solid reasons. This should not be politically interpreted as another minority appeasement measure."

The Kerala government had next tried to promote an Islamic finance institution, but the move was challenged in the High Court.

The RBI has now said that "given the complexities of Islamic finance and various regulatory and supervisory challenges involved, and also due to the fact that Indian banks have no experience in this field, Islamic banking may be introduced in a gradual manner".

"Initially, a few simple products which are similar to conventional banking products may be considered for introduction through Islamic window of the conventional bank. Introduction of full-fledged Islamic banking with profit-loss sharing complex products may be considered at a later stage on the basis of experience," the RBI has said. (The Indian Express, 2016)

5.6.1 Alternative Framework for Islamic Financial Institutions without Violations

An Alternative Framework for Islamic financial institutions has multiple alternatives which can be used to promote Islamic financing in India without violating R. B. I. regulation and Banking Act provisions. Scholars of Islamic banking will appreciate that if not pure banking, several financial and related services can be taken by those who desire to do profit and loss based activities in financial sector. Some of these are set out below:

1. Equity Funds (conditions prescribed in contrast for bank as trustee of any company)

2. Islamic Equity Funds

3. Safe Deposit Locker Services

4. Electronic Funds Transferring

5. Investment Advisory Services

6. Venture Capital Funds

7. Private Equity Funds –Equity Index Funds

8. Equity Financing as an Executor if bank acts as a trustee

9. Lease Financing Business

10. Hire purchase business

11. Discounting of bills and Vouchers on commission basis

12. Factoring services

13. Foreign Exchange Authorised Dealers Services

14. Foreign Travel Card Services

15. Initial Public offer Services

16. Merchant Banking Services

17. ATM Services

18. Broking Services

19. Infrastructure Financing as a Joint Venture

20. Demat Services

21. Custodian Services

22. Registrar & Transfer Agents

It is also possible for Islamic Institution to go for Joint financing of infrastructure projects with Government in this case the investment will be Shariah Compliant. Bank can present itself that it would assist investors in making long term investment in Shariah compliant way in infrastructure projects. Islamic Institution can also set up technical and professional educational / institutes on commercial basis. In order to achieve the above objectives Credit Societies and non deposit - NBFCs wholly owned by equity shareholders including foreign shareholders even by foreign participants should be promoted. There is a real need for a shared perspective and greater degree of accountability of executives including the board members. If Islamic financial institutions have to grow, they will have to observe several disciplines in order to protect the interest of their clients and other stakeholders from risk and uncertainties.

Islamic financial institutions have to be equally responsible to achieve financial stability through certain measures which are as follows:

I. Corporate Governance -Islamic financial services are fundamentally different from conventional financial services since Islamic financing emphasizes on equitable distribution of gains / losses between shareholders, depositors, borrowers, employees. So, corporate governance has manifold virtues to be obtained by Islamic Financial Organisation. Corporate governance is an age old recommendation of Islam even for a simple deal, either of financial nature or physical nature. Transparency, equitable distribution of profits, wages and other benefits, fair transactions are the bases of Sharia economic system that stresses on nurturing a moral affiliation between all stakeholders as well as fair treatment of clients, employees and suppliers. These days, the globally integrated financial market on the one hand, is the most competent institution as it is crowned with advanced technology which gets things done automatically, new financial products and services, extended market trading, technically strong players offering efficient services, and on the other hand it involves systematic as well as unsystematic risk, uncertainty, volatility, unpredictability. Financial market is the network which excites everyone to earn high returns but with high risk and high uncertainty. This eventually paves the way for economic agents working in a free market to use corrupt business practices, manipulations, fraud, and breach of trust, exploitation and unfair trade to maximize their wealth. It is here that mandatory corporate governance with Islamic ethics becomes a necessity for free markets with legal intervention being warranted as an integral part of the system. That is why Islamic financial organizations with a small capital base, mobilization deposits or savings on a meager scale from the middle class and weaker segments of society, particularly in countries like Bangladesh, India, Pakistan, Indonesia, Iran and other similar countries have to take extra care while utilizing the savings of small investors. India cannot provide a good example of Islamic banking and other financial services as of now and should learn lesson from such failures. The frame work of corporate governance comprises a number of constituencies like the Board of Directors, Audit Committee, Investment Committee, Shariah and Risk Management Committee. Moreover, financial expertise and accounting honesty will have to be pre-requisite of the executives for managing the financial services.

II. Management Accountability- The over-riding aim of executives should be to maximize the efficiency of the financial institution without being detrimental to the interest of the other employees. The management however, is subservient to the Board of Directors and must operate within the boundaries of the policy framework laid down by the Board. While the Board is responsible for ensuring that principles of governance of financial institutions are adhered to and enforced, the real onus of the implementation lies with the management. It is responsible for translating into action, the policies and strategies of the Board and implementing its directives to achieve corporate objectives of the financial institution framed by the Board. It is therefore essential that the Board should clearly define the role of management. The management according to Sunnah should have three fundamental qualities like honesty, accountability and transparency in functions. Islamic financial institutions have to be efficient in disclosure, monitoring and transparency and implementing Islamic tenets relating to financial activities. Internal control and overseeing of functions should be assigned to internal auditors by the management. Internal auditing is a necessity for recognizing and evaluating risk, detecting problems within the financial institution and correcting inconsistencies and deficiencies. An efficient auditing system would cover all on and off balance sheet functions of the financial institution and would indicate likely risk emerging in the financial institution. Good institutional authority directs a compulsion on the management with respect to disclosures. The management should be making the disclosures to the management related to all financial, material and commercial transactions, where they can have some personal interest which can conflict with the interest of the financial institution.

III. Investor's Protection: Conventional banks/institutes guarantee repayment of deposits as well as interest amount on deposits. Depositors of Islamic financial institution are fundamentally different as they deposit their savings with Islamic institutes on partnership basis and earn profit / loss and not fixed return and assured repayment of deposits. Thus depositors of Islamic financial institution participate in risk and uncertainty along with the financial institution's shareholders. In view of this aspect, depositors should be represented on the board of Directors and meetings of the shareholders. Financial institution executives should not resort to "adverse selection" approach to earn higher return from risky and unsound projects. Moral hazard is a result of weak ethical values. Promoters of closely held institutes should also refrain from high risk taking. They should serve as trustees of depositors. Islamic Financial Institutions have to adopt the following strategy for protection of depositors. Islam has recommended strict discipline of trustees who have to work as guarantors and protectors of depositors.

1. Islamic financial institution should have high capital adequacy ratios
2. They should constitute depositors and shareholders protection funds
3. They should constitute investment fluctuation reserves
4. Contingency reserve should be created to face unforeseen detrimental impact
5. Risk management strategies have to be resorted to without compromising on the interest of depositors.

IV. Risk Management: Management of risk is important in a business for its survival; more so in an Islamic bank as it is prescribed by the Sharia also. Not taking measures for the protection of wealth from certain risk is also one of the violations of Sharia. Thus it is recommended for an Islamic bank to set up a Risk management Committee for the management of credit and market risk.

The risk arising from over exposure to interconnected entities had been a threat for the existence of the financial institution in the past, thus the formation of a risk management committee should be strengthened in the institution.

The Risk committee should have arms length distance from executives involved in lending and investment. Financial Institutions, in the process are faced with various kinds of financial and non-financial risks like Credit risk, market risk (which includes foreign exchange risk, liquidity risk, equity price risk, commodity price risk legal risk, regulatory risk, reputational risk, operational risk etc). With the globalisation and liberalisation policies the entire financial system have become more integrated with the external markets, the risks thereof have become more complicated and require effective risk management. These risks are interrelated and thus can have an effect over a range of risk categories. Thus, Islamic institutions should have a careful assessment to measure, identify, monitor and control the overall risk.

In this context, Islamic financial institutions including banks are required to address all material kinds of risks in a planned way by advancement of their risk management skills and adopting more wide-ranging risk management practices.

The spectrum in which risk management should be working is:

1. Organisational structure
2. Comprehensive risk management approach
3. Risk management policies approved by the board which should be consistent with the broader business strategies, capital strength, management expertise and overall willingness to assume risk
4. Guidelines and other parameters used to govern risk taking including detailed structure of prudential limits
5. Strong MIS for reporting, monitoring and controlling risks
6. Well laid down procedures, effective control and comprehensive risk reporting framework
7. Separate risk management strategy division independent of operational department and with clear delineation of levels of responsibility.
8. Islamic institutions which are large in size can think of integrated risk.

9. Periodical review and evaluation. Due to the diversity and varying size of balance sheet items between financial institutions, it cannot be considered feasible or necessary for them to adopt a uniform risk management system.

Therefore, Islamic financial institutions are advised that the plan of risk management framework should be in line with the institutions' own necessity as per the size and the complexity of business, market perception, risk philosophy and existing level of capital. The primary responsibility of highlighting the risk factors and establishment of the risk management and control system should be vested with the board of directors. However, the risk management committee or a committee of top executives will have to report to the board. Islamic institutions have to constitute a high level investment policy committee to deal with issues pertaining to loan sanction, disbursement, investment in equity, dividend linked bonds units of equity and interest free units of mutual funds, leasing and other assets including all balance sheet items. They should have follow-up procedures to manage and control credit risk. This committee will ensure compliance of the risk factors and important limits set by the board and its monitoring too. In some countries it was revealed during the financial crises that there was a strong correlation between un-hedged market risk and credit risk. There should be integration between the activities of asset-liability management and management of credit and market risks.

Risk management needs to be focussed to construct a viable and sustainable network of financial services which should be Sharia complaint as well as financially strong.

5.6.2 Islamic Banking Framework in Current Banking Regulation

As discussed above, Islamic banks in India cannot function under the banking regulations as per the Banking Regulation Act described in Chapter 3. They are licensed under Non Banking Finance Companies Reserve Bank Directives 1997 RBI (Amendment) Act 1997, as NBFCs and function on PLS based on Islamic principles. As per the Monetary and Credit Policy for the year 1999-2000, it was proposed that "in respect of new NBFCs, which seek registration with the RBI and commence the business on or after April 21, 1999, the requirement of minimum level of net owned funds will be Rs 2 crore". For passing Islamic Banking, the Central Bank has to work out the proper framework to suit Islamic banking as it requires sharing of profit and loss as per the PLS system, with depositors and investors, apart from certifying that the funds act in accordance with with RBI and SEBI rules.

Sharia finance through Co-operative Societies

As of today there are certain regulations mentioned before which does not allow full fledged Islamic banking, even then it can be practiced to a limited extent without violating the government regulations. Financial products which are free can be practiced under Co-operative Credit Society by the members of the society for themselves. Such societies are regulated by the RBI and are governed by Central Registrar of Co-operative Credit Societies when it is present in a number of states. These societies are developed for the purpose of serving individuals or a group of people who belong to low or medium income group, and who do not have access to bank's loans as banks consider risk factors and creditworthiness of the applicant for the approval of loan for the applicant.

Co-operative Society can be defined as "a union of persons established according to the principles of equality, the purpose is to improve the financial position of its members by joint performance, provided that all profits made; aim to distribute among the members".

Literally the word co-operation is derived from the Latin word co-operari in which the word co means 'with' and operari means 'to work'. So the real meaning of co-operation is 'working together'. People who want to work together for achieving a common goal can form a society which is known as co-operative society. For this purpose, Co-operative Credit Society is made to provide credit to its members, and the society accepts deposits from the members and grant loans to them at reasonable cost.

A number of Co-operative Credit Societies are working with the interest free principle in India and are registered under "Multi State Co-operative Societies Act,2002" like Al-Khair Cooperative Credit Society Ltd which is Patna based and has its operations in 4 states. Janseva Co-operative Credit Society Ltd which is Mumbai based is working in 12 states in India.

"Janseva Co-operative Credit Society Limited" is working with its 23 Branches in India, and have membership of around 16000 members, with the paid up share capital of about Rs. 4 crores since 15thMarch' 2010, and has completed six years of existence.

Janseva Co-operative Society has been offering a number of Sharia compliant products and services to its members like Savings Account, investment and deposits, Loans and Recurring deposits, trade and investment plans, Hajj Fund Deposit, Self Help group Fund, Children Education Fund, Mutual Help Loan Group Fund,etc. For encouraging the habit of saving among its members Janseva has offered products like Amanah Saving Fund (ASF), Amanah Daily Fund Deposit (ADF) and the Amanah Compensatory Loan Fund (ACLF). Janseva has a good number of innovative products for investment and trading loans.

In India the Islamic finance needs an environment to grow and it is possible only with the support of the community's initiatives to give it a chance to prove. There should be community awareness of Sharia compliant products and services should be motivated. Awareness of such co-operative societies needs to be done so that more and more people should join this initiative and make it a success.

(Humble, 2015, Muslim mirror)

After the discussion of the expected role of Islamic banking in India, its challenges and the expected framework in the present chapter, it was felt necessary to elaborate the prospects of Islamic banking in India which has been made the subject matter of the next chapter.

CHAPTER-6
PROSPECTS OF ISLAMIC BANKING IN INDIA

In this chapter the data collected was analyzed by testing of hypotheses. It explores the awareness, attitude of people towards Islamic Banking in India based on 311 respondents in which 157 were Muslims and 154 were other communities to ascertain the prospects of zero interest based system known as Islamic banking in India.

6.1 Pilot Study

As the questionnaire was developed in line with the previous researches there is a need to test the questionnaire for its reliability with the said sample and in present times. There were 50 questions including demographic variables a sample of 60 respondents was selected for the purpose. Respondents were required to mention the items that were difficult to understand specially the terms which were in Arabic, so an explanation in one line was provided in the questionnaire explaining the Arabic term in English for ease of understanding for the respondents.

Reliability of the Test

Reliability refers the degree of consistency in multiple measurements of variables. An instrument is said to be reliable when any test or measuring procedure yields the same result after repeated attempts. Internal consistency in the variables in a summated scale gives an estimate of reliability. Cronbach's alpha is a co-efficient of reliability. Cronbach's alpha may be defined as a function of the number of test matters and the average inter-correlation between the items. The formula for the standardized Cronbach's alpha:

$$\alpha = \frac{N \cdot \bar{c}}{\bar{v} + (N-1) \cdot \bar{c}}$$

in this situation N refers the frequency of items, c-bar is the average inter-item covariance between the items and v-bar equals the average variance. One may conclude from the above formula that if the number of items gets increased, then Cronbach's alpha also gets increased. Besides, if average inter-item correlation is lower, then the alpha will also be lower and if there is an increase in the correlation of the items the Cronbach's alpha will also increase (holding the number of items constant). (UCLA)

Cronbach's alpha coefficient of reliability was used based on primary data of the present study and the details are as follows:

1. **Reliability Analysis of the Variable Awareness Item Wise**

   Table: 6.1 Reliability Analysis of the Variable Awareness Item Wise

Items	Scale Mean if Item Deleted	Scale Variance if Item Deleted	Corrected Item-Total Correlation	Squared Multiple Correlation	Cronbach's Alpha if Item Deleted
Awareness of Islamic banks	33.7333	70.606	.333	.359	.850
IB are based on Sharia	33.3167	71.542	.379	.504	.846
Riba prohibited in Islam	33.4000	73.668	.162	.536	.860
Awareness of Mudarabah	34.5833	61.501	.693	.775	.824
Awareness of Musharakah	34.5000	63.847	.653	.836	.828
Awareness of Musharakah	34.8500	63.350	.685	.780	.825
Awareness of Bai Muajjal	35.0500	64.286	.684	.593	.826
Awareness of Bai Salam	34.9833	60.932	.763	.760	.818
Awareness of Istisna	35.0667	61.385	.790	.809	.817
Awareness of Ijarah	34.8667	60.490	.796	.777	.816
QardHasan	34.9333	63.792	.547	.581	.836
No knowledge	35.2333	79.979	-.166	.214	.885

Source: Compiled by researcher from questionnaire filled by respondents

2. Reliability Analysis of Motivational Factors Item Wise

Table 6.2 Reliability analysis of Motivational Factors item wise

Items	Scale Mean if Item Deleted	Scale Variance if Item Deleted	Corrected Item-Total Correlation	Squared Multiple Correlation	Cronbach's Alpha if Item Deleted
Interest free methods	50.2000	87.180	.568	.704	.902
According to Sharia	50.3167	86.559	.502	.775	.904
Realisation of variable returns	51.3000	81.264	.676	.715	.897
Religious motivation for depositing	50.6333	88.677	.365	.677	.909
CoB not fixed	51.2000	83.688	.570	.545	.902
Mudarabah Investment	51.0833	84.078	.621	.571	.900
Repayment as per condition	50.8333	82.989	.622	.612	.900
Musharakah Lending	50.9333	80.131	.774	.749	.893
Sharing of Business risk	51.0500	84.218	.545	.560	.903
Business Support frm IB	50.8667	83.338	.687	.768	.897
Encourages innovation	50.7500	84.123	.671	.841	.898
Improves business efficiency	50.8500	83.316	.655	.862	.898
Provide lease finance	50.9833	81.881	.668	.758	.898
trade financing	50.9667	84.134	.603	.683	.900

Source: Compiled by researcher from questionnaire filled by respondents

3. Reliability Analysis of Attitude of People Item Wise

Table 6.3 Reliability Analysis of Attitude of People Item Wise

Items	Scale Mean if Item Deleted	Scale Variance if Item Deleted	Corrected Item-Total Correlation	Cronbach's Alpha if Item Deleted
Limited scope	21.1333	12.219	.039	.396
Only educated people switch	20.9667	10.677	.230	.270
IB Returns acceptable	20.2167	10.342	.485	.149
Complete faith will opt IB	21.0333	11.965	.099	.354
Performance better in meltdown	20.2333	12.995	.047	.374
IB services diversified	20.3667	11.524	.286	.256
Will have majority of population	20.7500	12.733	.013	.404

Source: Compiled by researcher from questionnaire filled by respondents

4. Reliability Analysis of Variable Implementation Item Wise

Table: 6.4 Reliability Analysis of Variable Implementation Item Wise

Items	Scale Mean if Item Deleted	Scale Variance if Item Deleted	Corrected Item-Total Correlation	Cronbach's Alpha if Item Deleted
Implement Mudarabah	30.8750	70.723	.629	.785
Implement Musharakah	30.6667	68.841	.701	.777
Implement Murabaha	30.6667	73.101	.558	.792
Implement BaiMuajjal	31.5833	69.210	.770	.773
Implement BAi Salam	31.4583	70.868	.725	.778
Implement Istisna	31.7083	69.520	.793	.772
Implement Ijara	31.7500	71.065	.745	.777
Implement Qard Hasana	31.1667	75.884	.435	.804
No implementation of Islamic finance	30.6667	89.884	-.117	.846
Using interest	32.0417	82.476	.233	.818
Give in charity	30.5417	78.085	.298	.818
Int free schemes	29.9583	89.694	-.108	.843

Source: Compiled by researcher from questionnaire filled by respondents

5. Reliability Analysis of Variable Application Item Wise

Table 6.5 Reliability Analysis of variable Application item wise

Items	Scale Mean if Item Deleted	Scale Variance if Item Deleted	Corrected Item-Total Correlation	Cronbach's Alpha if Item Deleted
Use IB	24.9583	19.085	.828	.895
More people	25.2083	18.694	.811	.897
No profit condition	25.2917	19.259	.803	.898
Helping community	25.4167	21.123	.640	.914
Safer IB	25.2917	21.520	.696	.910
More Investment	25.2917	19.694	.742	.904
Employment	25.5417	19.824	.701	.909

Source: Compiled by researcher from questionnaire filled by respondents

Table 6.6 Overall Reliability Measures of the Study

S.NO.	Variable	No. of Items	Cronbach's Alpha
1.	Awareness	12	.847
2.	Motivational Factors	14	.907
3.	Attitude	7	.355
4.	Application	12	.815
5	Implementation	7	.917
6.	Overall reliability	52	.880

Source: Compiled by researcher from questionnaire filled by respondents

A reliability coefficient of .70 or higher is considered "acceptable" in most social science research situations. (UCLA)

6.2 Analysis of Response for Islamic Banking in India

The questionnaire administered in the study was pretested among 60 respondents as mentioned in the chapter 2 of the study. The awareness, attitude, impact of education level, motivating factors, implementation of Islamic Banking have been discussed in detail using various tools with the help of IBM SPSS Version-21. Test of ANOVA and t-test were used to study the prospects of Islamic banking in India. Descriptive statistics is used to understand the profile of the sample and to study

The influence of socio economic variables on the level of awareness and the perceptions towards Islamic banking can be seen in the sample area. This can also pave the way to understanding the demographic and socio-economic back grounds of the sample and their influence on the level of awareness on banking and financial products in general and Islamic banking practices in particular. This is carried out using percentage analysis and weighted average mean. The T-test was used to study the difference in the level of awareness between the two elements of sample that is Muslims and Other communities

$$t = \frac{\overline{X}_T - \overline{X}_C}{\sqrt{\frac{var_T}{n_T} + \frac{var_C}{n_C}}}$$

Formula for the t-test.

The condition for t-value to be positive is if the first mean is larger than the second and negative if it is smaller. To compute the t-value a table of significance is referred to test whether the ratio is big enough to say that the difference between the groups is not likely to have been a chance finding. To test the significance, a risk level is set called the alpha level. In most of the social researches, the "rule of thumb" is to set the alpha level at .05. This means that five times out of a hundred a statistically significant difference between the means would be found out even if there was none (i.e. by chance). Degrees of freedom also need to be determined. In the t-test the degrees of freedom is the sum of the persons in both groups minus 2. Given the alpha level, the df, and the t-value, can be found out in a standard table of significance to determine whether the t-value is large enough to be significant. If it is, it can be concluded that the difference between the means for the two groups is different. (Even given the variability).

One Way ANOVA test

"For measuring the difference of education level in having an impact on the preference of Islamic Banking among Muslims in India test of Anova was used. The one-way analysis of variance (ANOVA) is used to determine whether there are any significant differences between the means of three or more independent (unrelated) groups. The one-way ANOVA compares the means between the groups and determines whether any of those means are significantly different from each other. Usually, it is used to test the null hypothesis:

$$H_0: \mu_1 = \mu_2 = \mu_3 = \cdots = \mu_k$$

where μ = group mean and k = number of groups. If, however, the one-way ANOVA returns a significant result, we accept the alternative hypothesis (HA), which is that there are at least 2 group means that are significantly different from each other.

It is important to realize that the one-way ANOVA is a compilation test statistic and cannot tell which specific groups were significantly different from each other only that at least two groups were. To determine which specific groups differed from each other, a post hoc test is used. Because post hoc tests are run to confirm where the differences occurred between groups, they should only be run when an overall significant difference in group means (i.e., a significant one-way ANOVA result) is shown. Post-hoc tests attempt to control the experiment wise error rate (usually alpha = 0.05) in the same manner that the one-way ANOVA is used, instead of multiple t-tests. Post-hoc tests are termed a posteriori tests; that is, performed after the event (the event in this case being a study)".(Laerd)

6.3 Demographic Profile of the Respondents in the Sample

Table 6.7 Gender Classification of Respondents

Respondent's Gender	N	Percent
Female	114	36.7
Male	197	63.3
Total	311	100.0

Source: Computed by researcher from primary data collected

Fig. 6.1 Gender Classification of Respondents

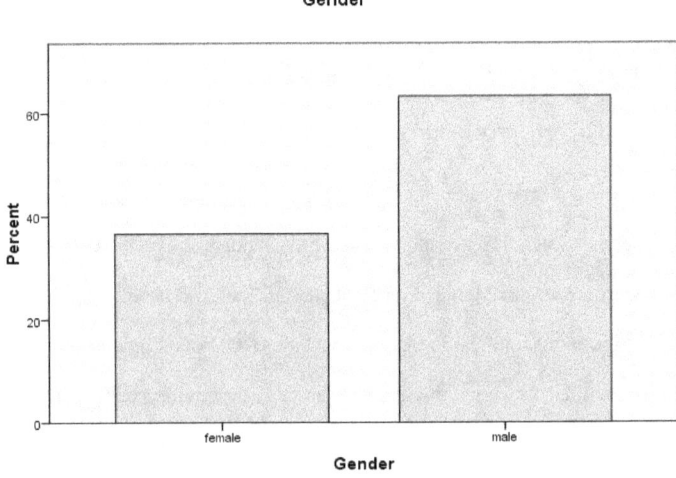

Source: Computed by researcher from primary data collected

It is observed from the Table 6.7 that 63.3% of respondents were male while the rest 36.7% were female. It clearly shows that financial empowerment of the female population in the sample area is less as compared to men.

Table: 6.8 Classification of Respondents on the basis of Age

Age Group (in years)	N	Percent
<25	23	7.4
26-35	237	76.2
36-45	41	13.2
46-55	9	2.9
56 or above	1	.3
Total	311	100.0

Source: Computed by researcher from primary data collected

Fig. 6.2 Classification of Respondents on the basis of Age

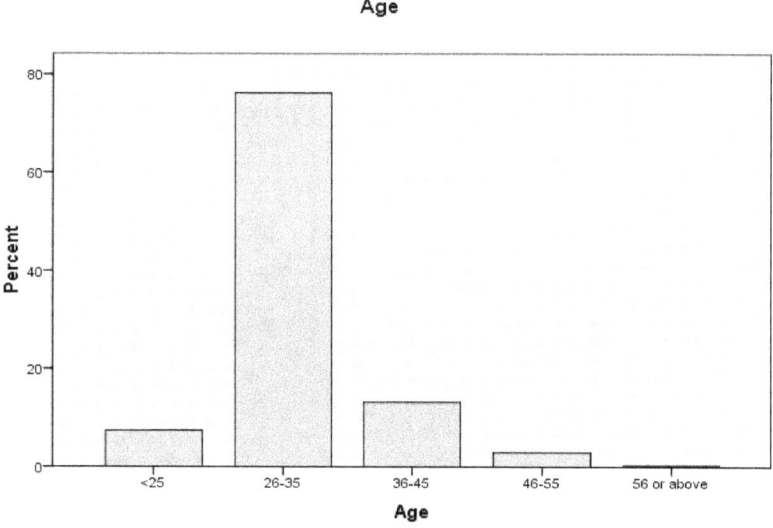

Source: Computed by researcher from primary data collected

It is observed from the Table 6.8 of Age category 76.2% belong to age group of 26-35 years. The age group 18-25 comprised of 7.4 % of the sample. The rest of the distribution was 36-45 years had 13.2% of presence. 46-55 years as 2.9% and 56 or above years of age had 0.3%.

Table 6.9 Classification of Respondents on the basis of Educational Qualifications

Education	N	Valid Percent
UG	18	5.8
Graduate	17	5.5
PG	216	69.5
Doctorate or above	60	19.3
Total	311	100.0

Source: Computed by researcher from primary data collected

Fig: 6.3 Classification of Respondents on the basis of Educational Qualifications

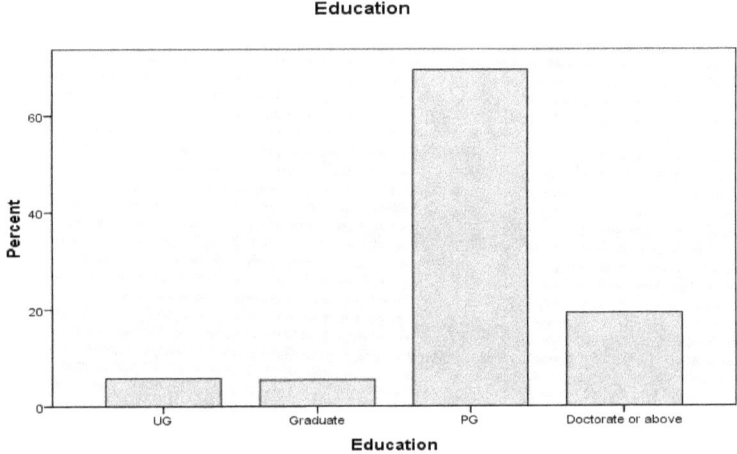

Source: Computed by researcher from primary data collected

The sample had respondents in which 69.5% were Post Graduate, 19.3% had a degree of Doctorate or above, Under Graduates were 5.8% and Graduates were 5.5% as can be seen in Table: 6.9.

Table: 6.10 Classification of Respondents on the basis of Occupation

Occupation	N	Valid Percent
Public	20	6.4
Private	186	59.8
Self Employed	23	7.4
Student	31	10.0
Others	51	16.4
Total	311	100.0

Source: Computed by researcher from primary data collected

Fig: 6.4 Classification of Respondents on the basis of Occupation

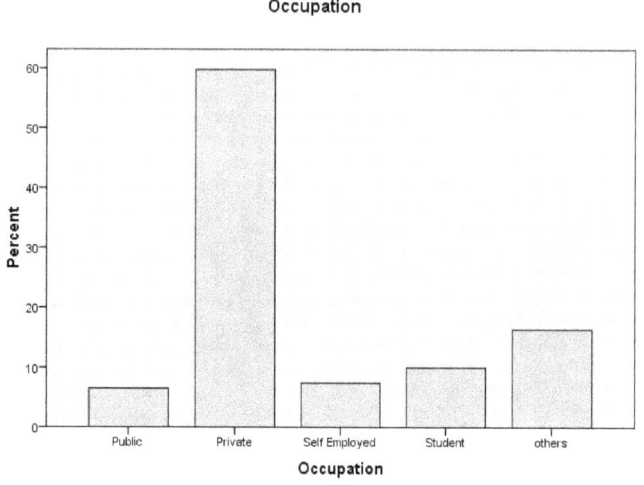

Source: Computed by researcher from primary data collected

The sample consisted of 59.8% of private employees, 6.4% were in Public Sector, 7.4% were self employed, 10% were students and 16.4% belonged to others category as can be seen in Table 6.10.

Table: 6.11 Classification of Respondents on the basis of Religion

Religion	N	Percent
Muslim	157	50.5
Other communities	154	49.5
Total	311	100.0

Source: Computed by researcher from primary data collected

Fig.6.5 Classification of Respondents on the basis of Religion

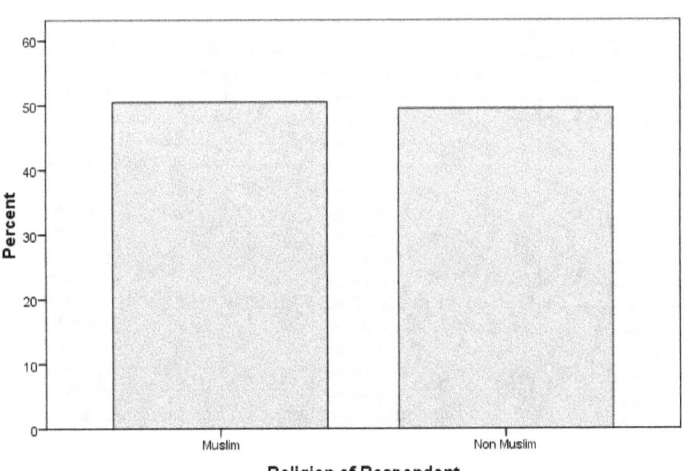

Source: Computed by researcher from primary data collected

The sample was categorized in Muslim and people from other communities while Muslims were 50.5% and People from other communities were 49.5% which is almost at par with Muslims in the said sample. So both the respondents have almost equal representation as can be seen in Table:6.11.

6.4 Testing of Hypotheses

6.4.1 H_{01}: There is no significant difference in awareness of Islamic banking among Muslims and people from other communities.

For testing the above hypothesis of the study t test was used to measure the difference in the level of awareness between the two elements of sample that is Muslims and people from other communities in the country which reveals the following results:

Table: 6.12: Assessing awareness of Islamic Banking

Category	N	Mean	SD	t-Value	Sig.(2-tailed)
Muslims	157	36.2102	9.24664	19.460	0.000*
People from other communities	154	18.0455	7.04453		

Source: Computed by researcher from primary data collected, *Significant at 0.000 level.

Therefore, hypothesis 1 is rejected that is there is no significant difference in awareness of Islamic Banking amongst Muslims and people from other communities.
But it was also observed that in certain questions related to products like Musharakah, Bai Muajjal, Bai salam. In such questions both the groups showed lack of knowledge.

Fig.6.6 Awareness of Bai Muajjal

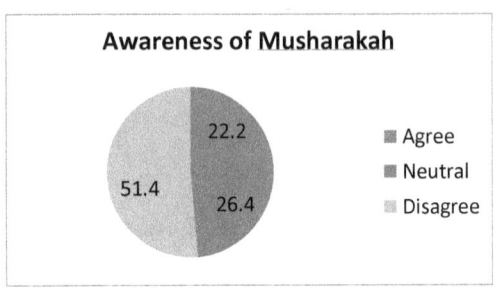

Source: Computed by researcher from primary data collected

It can be seen from Fig.6.6 the awareness of Musharakah in the selected sample is less as when asked about its awareness 22.2% agreed that they are aware about it, 51.4% disagreed and 26.4% had no opinions.

Fig: 6.7 Awareness of Bai Muajjal

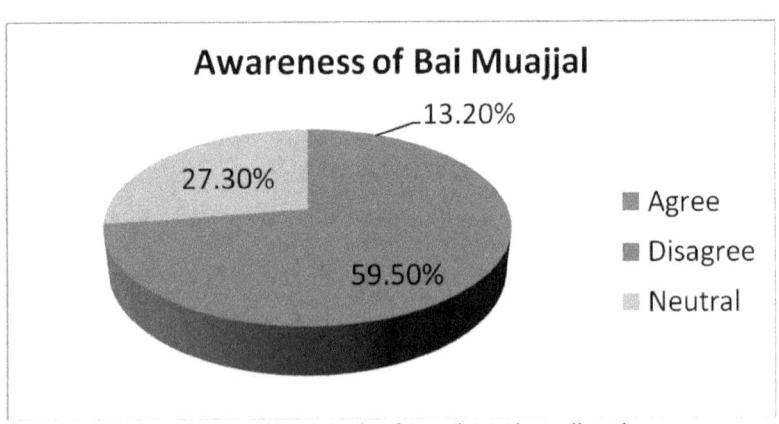

Source: Computed by researcher from primary data collected

It can be seen from Fig.6.7 the awareness of Bai Muajjal in the selected sample is less as when asked about its awareness 13.2% agreed that they are aware about it, 59.5% disagreed and 27.3% had no opinions.

6.4.2 H_{02}: There is no difference of education level over preference or attitude of interest free methods of banking.

For measuring difference of education level in having an impact on the preference of Islamic Banking among Muslims in India test of Anova was used.

Table: 6.13: Assessing Impact of Education level in application of Islamic Banking.

ANOVA					
Impact of Education level	Sum of Squares	Df	Mean Square	F	Sig.
Between Groups	867.344	3	289.115	10.877	.000*
Within Groups	8160.116	307	26.580		
Total	9027.460	310			

Source: Computed by researcher from primary data collected, *Significant at 0.000 level.

Table: 6.14 Difference of attitude in different groups of education

Student-Newman-Keuls			
		Subset for alpha = 0.05	
Education	N	1	2
SSSC	18	14.4444	
PG	216		20.5972
Doctorate or above	60		21.2167
Graduate	17		23.7059
Sig.		1.000	.055

Source: Computed by researcher from primary data collected
Means for groups in homogeneous subsets are displayed.

When post hoc (SNK test) was applied to check the difference among groups, it was found that those who were at senior secondary level (Mean=14.44) were different from higher education groups (Graduate, PG, Doctorate) (Mean=23.7,20.6,21.2)

Therefore, hypothesis 2 is rejected that is there is a significant difference of education level over preference or attitude towards interest free banking methods.

6.4.3 H_{03}: There is no difference in application of Islamic banking methods among Muslims and people from other communities.

Islamic banking methods can be applied in day to day financial transactions by avoiding interest in banking and other dealings as well. The above hypothesis was put to test and the following results were found.

Table: 6.15 Difference in application of Islamic banking methods among Muslims and people from other communities

Category	N	Mean	SD	t-Value	Sig.(2-tailed)
Muslims	157	32.8535	9.81875	9.947	0.000*
People from other communities	154	22.1818	9.07878		

Source: Computed by researcher from primary data collected, *Significant at 0.000 level.

Thus seeing the results *hypothesis 3 is rejected that is there a significant difference in application of Islamic banking methods among Muslims and people from other communities.*

6.4.4 H_{A4}: Muslims are giving in charity the interest which they receive from banks.

Table: 6.16 Muslims are giving in charity the interest received from the banks or not

Category	N	Mean	SD	t-Value	Sig.(2-tailed)
Giving in charity	157	3.4268	1.46	29.50	0.000*

Source: Computed by researcher from primary data collected, *Significant at 0.000 level.

Muslims in the group were asked about how they have been utilizing interest which they receive from commercial banks most of them mentioned of giving in charity the amount of interest with the t value of 29.50 which is significant at 0.000 levels. *Thus hypothesis 4 is accepted that Muslims are giving in charity the interest received from banks.*

6.4.5 H_{A5} Muslims are taking measures to avoid interest by not investing in interest laden schemes.

Muslims are taking measures to avoid interest by not investing in interest laden schemes.

I ensure that the schemes I choose for investment should be interest free.

Table: 6.17 Muslims are taking measures to avoid interest

Responses	Frequency	Percent
Strongly Disagree	21	13.4
Disagree	9	5.7
Neutral	27	17.2
Agree	36	22.9
Strongly Agree	64	40.8
Total	157	100.0

Source: Computed by researcher from primary data collected

Fig. 6.8 Muslims are taking measures to avoid interest

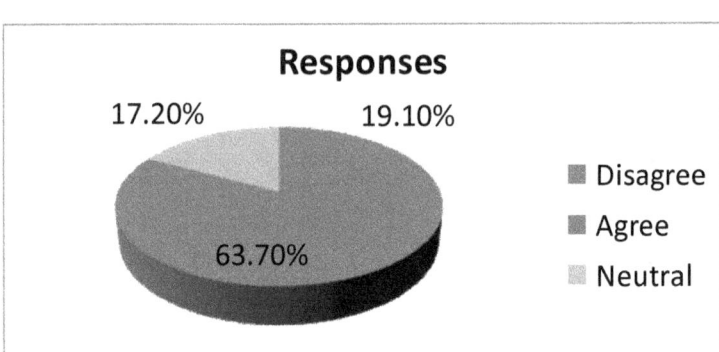

Source: Computed by researcher from primary data collected

By combining the responses of Strongly Agree and Agree it was found that 63.8% Muslims were ensuring that the schemes which they use for investment purpose should be interest free.19.10% disagreed and 17.2% had no opinion.

Thus, Hypothesis 5 is accepted as majority of Muslims are not investing in interest laden schemes.

6.4.6 H06: There is no difference in getting affected by motivating factors of Islamic Banking in India amongst Muslims and Others.

Table: 6.18 Difference of getting affected by motivating factors of Islamic banking in Muslims and Others

Category	N	Mean	SD	t-Value	Sig.(2-tailed)
Muslims	157	55.49	8.74	13.42	0.000*
Others	154	40.34	11.04		

Source: Computed by researcher from primary data collected, *Significant at 0.000 level.

Muslims and Others were compared using t-test to know the difference of effect of motivating factors of Islamic Banking. From the above table it was observed that Other communities (Mean=40.34; SD=11.04) and Muslims having (Mean=55.49; SD=8.74) have significant difference at 0.000 levels with t-value of 13.42. *Thus, the hypothesis 6 is rejected and there is a significant difference in effect of motivating factors of Islamic banking among Muslims and respondents from other communities.*

6.5 Observations in the Study

It is interesting to note that some respondents from other communities are also ready to try interest free banking as can be seen through their response to the questions like.

MF-3 "Realisation of higher and variable rate of return on deposits whether it is a motivating factor for people towards Islamic Banking or not", 53.24% of respondents of other communities responded positively.

MF-5 "Cost of borrowing not being fixed but depending on the outcome of the business", whether it is a motivating factor for people towards Islamic Banking, 52.64% of respondents of other communities responded positively.

Fig. 6.9 CoB Not fixed but dependent on outcome of the business.

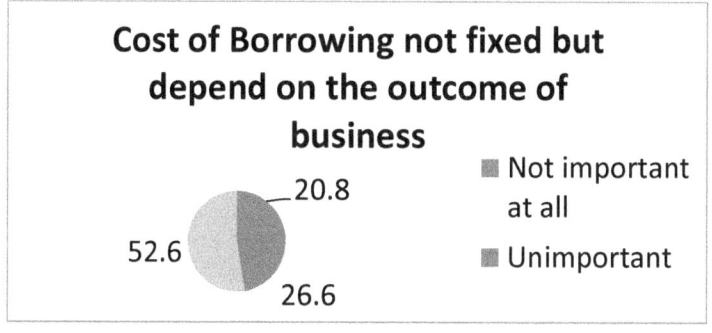

Source: Computed by researcher from primary data collected

Fig. 6.10 Repayment of debt

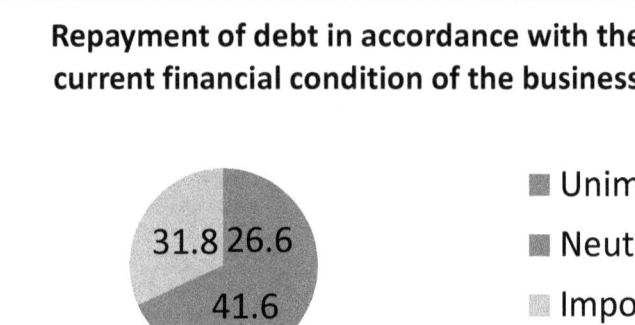

Source: Computed by researcher from primary data collected

IM1- If Islamic banks open up in India; I would like to use their Islamic methods of finance. To the above question 11% of Respondents of other communities were positive. 62.3% were neutral and 26.6% were negative. This shows their interest in Islamic banking although smaller in number but still they would like to know the concept.

IM6- If interest free banking facilities are being provided in India it will create more investment opportunities for interest avoiding people from abroad and within the country.

To this question regarding implementation 25.32% of people responded positively. Some more observations were made like:

Table: 6.19 Practice of Qard hasana

Responses	Frequency	Valid Percent
Strongly Disagree	135	43.4
Disagree	27	8.7
Neutral	105	33.8
Agree	27	8.7
Strongly Agree	17	5.5
Total	311	100.0

Source: Computed by researcher from primary data collected

Fig.6.11 Practice Qard Hasan

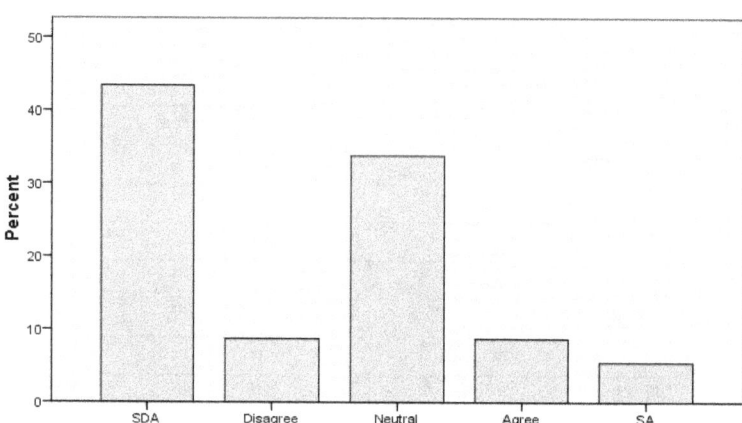

Source: Computed by researcher from primary data collected

It has been observed from The Table 6.19 and the Graph that 51.1% population of the sample denied of practicing benevolent loans and 33.8% were neutral and 14.2% agreed practicing benevolent loans (Qard Hasan) which is one of the practices of Islamic Banking.

Table 6.20 Level of Awareness of terminologies of Islamic Methods of finance and banking

Terminologies		Not at all aware	Not Aware	Neutral	Aware	Highly Aware	Total	Mean	SD
Musharakah	N	93	67	82	38	35	311	2.5	1.3
	%	29.5	21.3	21.5	12.2	15.5	100		
Mudarabah	N	100	66	76	43	30	311	2.5	1.3
	%	31.7	21.9	24.1	13.8	8.5	100		
Riba	N	101	9	56	49	96	311	**3.09**	1.64
	%	32.5	2.9	18	15.8	30.9	100		
Sharia	N	96	39	25	61	90	311	**3.03**	1.64
	%	30.9	12.5	8	19.6	28.9	100		
Bai Muajjal	N	138	47	85	28	13	311	2.13	1.2
	%	44.4	15.1	27.3	9	4.2	100		
Bai Salam	N	139	69	48	42	13	311	2.10	1.2
	%	44.7	22.2	15.4	13.5	4.2	100		
Istisna	N	141	46	74	39	11	311	2.14	1.2
	%	45.3	14.8	23.8	12.5	3.5	100		
Ijara	N	110	37	103	46	15	311	2.4	1.2
	%	35.4	11.9	33.1	14.8	4.8	100		
Qard Hasana	N	75	103	78	30	25	311	2.4	1.2
	%	24.1	33.1	25.1	9.6	8	100		

Source: Computed by researcher from primary data collected

From the above table 6.20 it can be observed that the general awareness of the terms of Islamic methods of Banking and finance it was observed that terms like Riba and Sharia recorded a higher mean that is 3.09 and 3.03 while other terms related to different methods of Islamic Finance recorded lower Mean score. This is because these terminologies are a part of the Islamic banking parlance and is not used even among the well-learned Muslims. Further, since there are no Islamic banks operational in India, as of now, it is not surprising that the awareness level for these terms is very low.

With these observations from the sample of the study it can be concluded that Muslims need an alternative banking system to follow their faith and practice their religion as the Constitution of India also gives us this freedom, and it will be acceptable by Other communities as well as all will benefit from the system which is free from reins of interest.

To see the percentages of Muslims who are utilizing interest from the survey it was found.

Table 6.21 Utilization of Interest

Responses	Frequency	Percent
Strongly Disagree	80	51.0
Disagree	24	15.3
Neutral	22	14.0
Agree	22	14.0
Strongly Agree	9	5.7
Total	157	100.0

Source: Computed by researcher from primary data collected

It can be observed from the above table 6.21 that approximately 66.3 % deny of utilizing the interest which they receive from the banks in their savings account.

Table: 6.22 Interest from commercial banks are given in charity

Responses	Frequency	Percent	Valid Percent	Cumulative Percent
Strongly disagree	28	17.8	17.8	17.8
Disagree	13	8.3	8.3	26.1
Neutral	29	18.5	18.5	44.6
Agree	38	24.2	24.2	68.8
Strongly Agree	49	31.2	31.2	100.0
Total	157	100.0	100.0	

Source: Computed by researcher from primary data collected

Fig. 6.12 Percentage of people utilizing the interest money for charity purpose

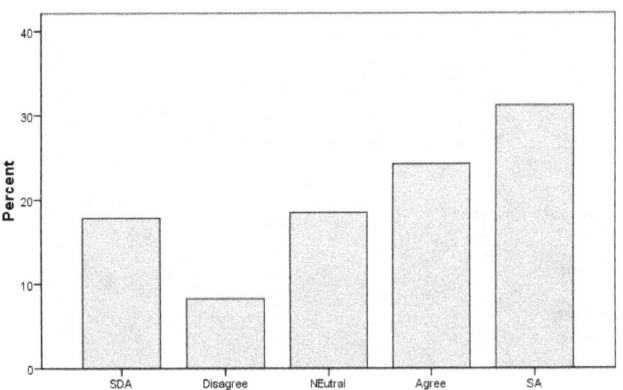

Source: Computed by researcher from primary data collected

Muslims numbering 157 were asked about their treatment of interest from commercial banks and the results reveal that 55.4% Muslims are taking out interest and giving in charity, 18.5 are neutral and 26.1% people disagree of giving interest in charity. So a major part of the Muslim population are not utilizing the interest from their commercial banks and giving away in charity.

Table: 6.23 People utilizing interest money for personal use

"I have been utilizing the interest from commercial banks or investments for personal use"

		Frequency	Percent	Valid Percent	Cumulative Percent
Valid	SDA	80	51.0	51.0	51.0
	Disagree	24	15.3	15.3	66.2
	Neutral	22	14.0	14.0	80.3
	Agree	22	14.0	14.0	94.3
	SA	9	5.7	5.7	100.0
	Total	157	100.0	100.0	

Source: Computed by researcher from primary data collected

Fig. 6.13 People utilizing interest money for personal use

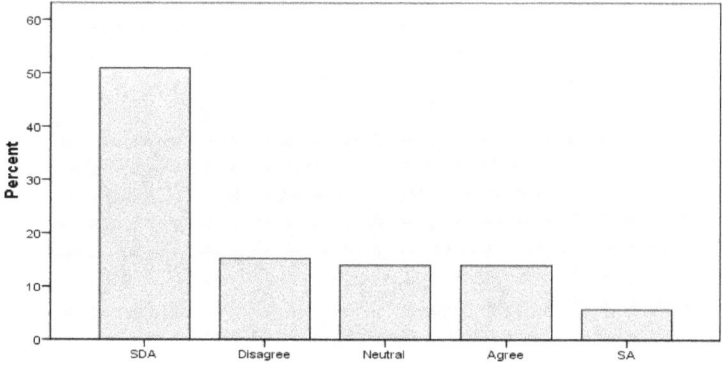

Source: Computed by researcher from primary data collected

Muslims numbering 157 were asked whether they are using the interest from commercial banks for personal use, the results reveal that 66.2% Muslims disagreed, 14% are neutral and 19.7% people agreed of utilizing interest. So a major part of the Muslim population is not utilizing the interest from their commercial banks.

Table 6.24 Preference to Interest free schemes for investment purpose

Responses	Frequency	Percent
Strongly Disagree	21	13.4
Disagree	9	5.7
Neutral	27	17.2
Agree	36	22.9
Strongly Agree	64	40.8
Total	157	100.0

Source: Computed by researcher from primary data collected

157 Muslims were asked whether they ensure that the schemes they choose for investment should be interest free 63.7% Muslims agreed that they choose only interest free schemes for investment and 19.1% disagreed and 17.2% had no opinion. This again implies that majority of Muslims are interest averse and they are making choices through which they can avoid interest.

Fig.6.14 Preference for Interest free Schemes

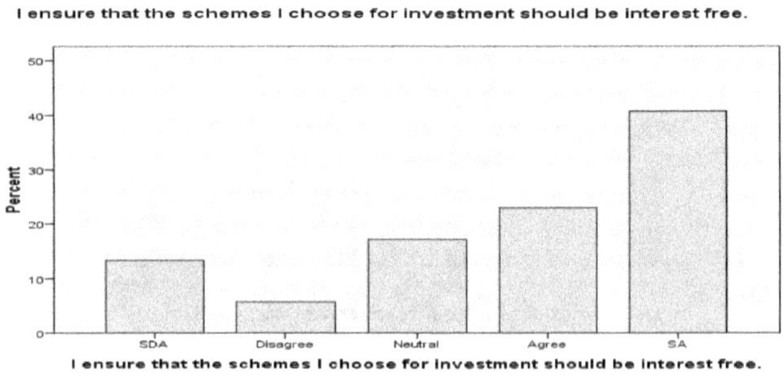

Source: Computed by researcher from primary data collected

As can be seen from Fig.6.14 that 63.7% of Muslims choose schemes which are interest free for investment, it is clear that Muslims are avoiding interest in some or the other form be it earnings interest from savings account or interest from investments made. Thus it is better that interest free schemes are chosen so that there is no question of interest earned from investments.

6.6 Sachar Committee for Economic Reforms of Depressed Sections

Sachar Committee in its report has also pointed out for economic upliftment of the Muslims by creating the framework which is giving the way for establishing interest free banking in the areas where the people in junk live and accept the interest free banking on Sharia principles of Islam. Some of the recommendations are enumerated below:

i) To set up an Equal Opportunity Commission to look into grievances of deprived groups like minorities.

ii) To create a nomination procedure to increase participation of minorities in public bodies.

iii) To establish a delimitation procedure that does not reserve constituencies with high minority population for SCs.

iv) To increase employment share of Muslims, particularly where there is great deal of public dealing. Work out mechanisms to link madarsas with higher secondary school board.

v) To recognise degrees from madarsas for eligibility in defence, civil and banking examinations.

vi) The Committee suggested that policies should "sharply focus on inclusive development and 'mainstreaming' of the Community while respecting diversity."

The Committee's mandate was to:

(a) "To obtain relevant information and conduct a literature survey on the relative social, economic an educational status of Muslims in India at the state, regional and district levels";

(b) "To determine the level of their socio-economic development";

(c) "To determine the relative share in public and private sector employment";

(d) "To determine the proportion of OBCs from Muslim community in the total OBC population in various states",

(e) "To determine access to education and health services, municipal infrastructure and bank credit provided by Government/ public sector entities".

By going through the report of Sachar Committee it is evident that Muslims in India need upliftment to bring them in the mainstream so that they can add into the progress of the country. The development of the nation is not possible by giving power to a few people or class, for the development and progress of the nation it is important that all its inhabitants are having a good quality life and thus they can contribute in the growth of the economy.

6.7 Financial Sector Reforms Committee on Financial Inclusion

The Committee on Financial Sector Reforms under the Chairmanship of the former Governor RBI Mr. Raghuram Rajan, 2007 has also mentioned about financial inclusion through interest free banking as can be seen from the excerpt of the report as follows:

"Another area that falls broadly in the ambit of financial infrastructure for inclusion is the provision of interest-free banking. Certain faiths prohibit the use of financial instruments that pay interest. The non-availability of interest-free banking products (where the return to the investor is tied to the bearing of risk, in accordance with the principles of that faith) results in some Indians, including those in the economically disadvantaged strata of society, not being able to access banking products and services due to reasons of faith. This non-availability also denies India access to substantial sources of savings from other countries in the region.

While interest-free banking is provided in a limited manner through NBFCs and cooperatives, the Committee recommends that measures be taken to permit the delivery of interest-free finance on a larger scale, including through the banking system. This is in consonance with the objectives of inclusion and growth through innovation. The Committee believes that it would be possible, through appropriate measures, to create a framework for such products without any adverse systemic risk impact."

Thus taking cues from the recommendations given in the committee it can be remarked that the prospects of Interest free banking in India is bright and it is the need of the hour to spread the banking services among the people who are not in the mainstream of banking and financial activities.

After the discussion on the prospects of Islamic banking in India on the basis of analysis of the response for the same in the present chapter, the next chapter presents the conclusions and suggestions made after conducting the present study. Moreover, the suggested areas for future research on Islamic banking have also been made the subject matter of the next chapter.

CHAPTER-7

CONCLUSION AND SUGGESTIONS

The present chapter is devoted to the discussion on major findings and conclusions of the study. Moreover, the suggestion made after conducting the present study, the scope for further studies and limitations of the study have also been discussed in the present chapter.

7.1 Findings and Conclusions

With this study it is observed that commercial banking is an age old practice in India and the entire financial system comprising of financial market, financial institutions, different financial instruments and financial services and the banking industry are interest based. The Indian financial system is divided into two constituents, first is comprised of organized banking and financial institutions and the second comprised of unorganized persons and institutions. The Reserve Bank of India is the central bank which controls all commercial banks, development banks, cooperative banks and other organized banking institutions coming under the definition of bank. Thus it is a difficult task to bring Islamic banking as all the rules and regulations are favouring the interest based economy. But presence of a fraction of population who is avoiding interest the entry of Islamic banking is possible.

Zero Interest based banking principles have a basis of the philosophies and principles outlined in the Quran and the Sunnah of Prophet Muhammad (Pbuh). So the terms which were used back then have been retained and some more concepts have been added for the present day sustenance. Thus Zero Interest based banking was very much there 1400 years ago. Today what is known as Islamic Banking came into existence around 1963. The Zero Interest based banking works on Profit and- Loss

Sharing (PLS) model which had been a pioneer in 1963 with the name of an Egyptian Savings Bank called as Mit Ghamr. Though, the very first commercial Zero Interest based bank of the world was considered to be Dubai Islamic Bank (DIB) which was founded in 1975. In India also there are people who are avoiding interest as can be seen from the findings of the study.

In the present study the prospects of Islamic banking was examined by a survey comprising of awareness of Islamic banking among the sample population, their attitude, the effect of motivating factors on them, the application of methods of Islamic finance in their day to day financial transactions, and their views on implementation of Islamic banking as explained in the findings of the study.

1. It can be concluded with the study that Muslims in India are more aware of Islamic Banking as compared to Non Muslims as the statistics show that there is a t-value of 19.460 which is significant at 0.000 levels. But it was also observed that in certain questions related to products like Musharakah, Bai Muajjal, Bai salam. In such questions both the groups showed lack of knowledge.

2. It was found that the difference in education level had an impact on the preference of Islamic Banking amongst the Muslims in India. With the use of post-hoc test it was found that the group who had qualifications as Graduate, PG, Doctorate was more inclined towards Islamic Banking as compared to the group which had qualification of an SSSC or Intermediate.

3. There is a significant difference in application of some general practices of Islamic Banking amongst Muslims and Non Muslims like

AP1-I have been practising the Islamic methods of finance myself (Mudarabah) only profit sharing

AP2-I have been practising the Islamic methods of finance myself (Musharakah) profit/loss sharing.

AP3-I have been practising the Islamic methods of finance myself (Murabahah)which is an acceptable form of credit sale under Sharia.

AP5-I have been practising the Islamic methods of finance myself (Bai Salam) a contract in which advance payment is made for goods to be delivered at a future date, following Islam and Islamic shariah.

AP8-I have been practising the Islamic methods of finance myself (Qard Hasan) benevolent loans.

AP11-Ihave been taking out the interest from commercial banks or investments and giving it in charity.

AP12-Iensure that the schemes I choose for investment should be interest free.

4. Muslims are more affected by motivating factors of Islamic banking as compared to Non Muslims which can be seen in the study where Muslims and Non Muslims were compared using t-test to know the difference of effect of motivating factors of Islamic Banking, it was observed that Non Muslims (Mean=40.34; SD=11.04) and Muslims having (Mean=55.49; SD=8.74) have significant difference at 0.000 levels with t-value of 13.42.

MF1 Interest free methods of finance.

MF2 Islamic methods of finance in accordance with Islamic Sharia

MF3 Realisation of higher and variable rate of return on deposits

MF4 Religious motivation for depositing/ borrowing with Islamic bank

5. It can also be concluded statistically through this study that majority of Muslims are not utilizing the interest for personal use which they receive from commercial banks as 66.3% of the Muslim population are not utilizing the

interest for personal use. 55.4% Muslims have been giving the interest from commercial banks in charity.

6. It is interesting to note that some Non Muslims are also ready to try interest free banking as can be seen through their response to the questions like.

MF3- Realisation of higher and variable rate of return on deposits, whether it is a motivating factor for people towards Islamic Banking, 53.24% of Non Muslims responded positively.

MF5- Cost of borrowing not being fixed but depending on the outcome of the business, whether it is a motivating factor for people towards Islamic Banking, 53.24% of Non Muslims responded positively.

IM1- If Islamic banks open up in India, I would like to use their Islamic methods of finance. To the above question 11% of Non Muslims respondents were positive. 62.3% were neutral and 26.6% were negative. This shows their interest in Islamic banking although smaller in number but still they would like to know the concept.

IM6- If interest free banking facilities are being provided in India it will create more investment opportunities for interest averse people from abroad and within the country.

To this question regarding implementation 25.32% of people responded positively.

With these observations from the sample of the study it can be concluded that Muslims need an alternative banking system to follow their faith and practice their religion as the Constitution of India also gives us this freedom, and it will be acceptable by Non Muslims as well as all will benefit from the system which is free from reins of interest. The major findings based on percentage analysis have been discussed in the ensuing paragraphs.

1. **Gender** - It is observed from the demographics of respondents that 63.3% were male while the rest 36.7% were female. It clearly shows that financial empowerment of the female population in the sample area is less as compared to men.

2. **Age-** It was observed that 76.2% belong to age group of 26-35 years. The age group 18-25 comprised of 7.4 % of the sample. The rest of the distribution was 36-45 years had 13.2% of presence. 46-55 years as 2.9% and 56 or above years of age had 0.3%. It indicates that the financial empowerment in the family is associated with the earning members and they fall in the age group of 26-35 years. The other reason could be that these respondents are conveniently approachable than the rest of the age group of the respondents. Age does play an important role in observing new concepts and ideas and also in implementing them. The level of financial awareness, in general, and decision making related to finance, in particular, may be more among the youth when compared to others in the sample.

3. **Educational Background-** The sample had respondents in which 69.5% were Post Graduate which formed the largest group in the sample, the second largest group was of 19.3% who had a degree of Doctorate or above, Under Graduates were 5.8% and Graduates were 5.5%.

4. **Religion-** The sample was categorized in Muslim and Non Muslim population while Muslims were 50.5% and Non Muslims were 49.5% which is almost at par with Muslims in the said sample. So both the respondents have almost equal representation.

5. **Occupation-** The sample consisted of 59.8% of private employees, 6.4% were in Public Sector, 7.4% were self employed, 10% were students and 16.4% belonged to others category.

6. **Practice of Qard Hasana-** It was observed that 51.1% population of the sample denied of practicing benevolent loans and 33.8% were neutral and 14.2% agreed practicing benevolent loans which is one of the practices of Islamic Banking. This showed that the practice of benevolent loans which is the very base of Islamic banking is practiced only among 14.2%. This is the data of overall sample.

   It was also observed that 28% of Muslim respondents agreed to practice Qard Hasana, 26.1% were neutral and 45.9% denied of practicing Qard Hasana. The reason for this might be that even Muslims are not aware of Islamic banking practices so they also do not practice it in their day to day life.

7. **Awareness of Terminologies-** It was observed that the general awareness of the terms of Islamic methods of Banking and finance it was observed that terms like Riba and Sharia recorded a higher mean that is 3.09 and 3.03 while other terms related to different methods of Islamic Finance recorded lower Mean score. This is because these terminologies are a part of the Islamic banking dialect and is not used even among the well-learned Muslims. Further, since there are no Islamic banks operational in India, as of now, it is not surprising that the awareness level for these terms is very low.

8. **Utilization of Interest by Muslims-** It was observed from the above table that approximately 66.3 % deny of utilizing the interest which they receive from the banks in their savings account. This shows that majority of Muslims have denied consumption of interest for personal use. It might be a different issue

that they might be giving interest earned from banks to charity but as they are holding accounts with the banks so it is quite obvious that they are receiving interest in their savings account, some may leave the interest in the bank or some may withdraw and give to some needy person. But this is an additional exercise which a Muslim who avoids interest has to perform with the commercial banking system.

9. **Interest from commercial banks or investments given in charity-** Muslims numbering 157 were asked about their treatment of interest from commercial banks and the results reveal that 55.4% Muslims are taking out interest and giving in charity, 18.5 are neutral and 26.1% people disagree of giving interest in charity. So a major part of the Muslim population are not utilizing the interest from their commercial banks and giving away in charity.

10. **Preference for interest free schemes for investment purpose-** 157 Muslims were asked whether they ensure that the schemes they choose for investment should be interest free 63.7% Muslims agreed that they choose only interest free schemes for investment and 19.1% disagreed and 17.2% had no opinion. This again implies that majority of Muslims are interest averse and they are making choices through which they can avoid interest.

It can be observed from the above findings that interest is avoided by major population of the sample. It is basically the demand of interest which makes the banks to pay interest to the deposits, if there is no demand of interest then banks will not have to pay interest and can operate smoothly even considering the risk premium, profit and cost of inflation. Thus the entire system can be made interest free just by removing the component of interest from the costs of the current commercial banks.

Economists and Philosophers have also pointed out a number of disadvantages of interest like The Greek philosopher, Aristotle, condemned acquiring of wealth by the practice of charging of interest on money.

"Very much disliked also is the practice of charging interest: and the dislike is fully justified for interest is a yield arising out of money itself, not a product of that for which money was provided. Money was intended to be a means of exchange; interest represents an increase in the money itself. Hence of all ways of getting wealth, this is the most contrary to nature." (Aristotle, The Politics, Penguin, 1995)

Also in other religious books interest is prohibited like "Do not charge your brother interest, whether on money or food or anything else that may earn interest." (Deuteronomy 23:19)

"If you lend money to My people, to the poor among you, you are not to act as a creditor to him; you shall not charge him interest." The Holy Bible
"If you have money, do not lend it at interest, but give it to one from whom you will not get it back." (Gospel St Thomas, V95).

It is just not disliked as it is in the religious books of people but also due to the fact that interest creates instability in the economy and by creating a gap between rich and the poor and with interest this gap becomes wider. These consequences have been highlighted by Mills (1993) as follows:

1. The unfair and destabilized distribution of returns among the users and suppliers of finance.
2. The unfair allocation of finances to the safest borrowers rather than the most productive ones
3. A tendency to finance speculation in assets and property.

4. An intrinsically unstable banking system which can only continue to exist with government guarantees.
5. A short term investment strategy.
6. The wealth being confined to fewer hands.
7. A rapid flow of financial capital across regions and countries where returns can be seen. Economic theory may believe that this will advance the efficiency of investment, but it contribute to the erosion of community and regional structure as jobs and opportunities have a propensity to follow flows of financial capital and thus can result in mass migrations.

So it is not only that Islam suggests that an interest free economy is more ethical and just but also Christianity and Jewish followers also have a similar thought about interest and thus there is no wonder that Zero Interest based banking is being widely accepted by other than Muslims as well. It is important to study and analyse the different models, concepts and notions which can be implemented in a country like India.

It is no wonder that Islamic Banking is being adopted by a number of countries as it is being considered more ethical, stable, fair, form of banking as compared to the traditional banking. In the Gulf interest free banks, in terms of their assets has one quarter of the industry and has share in single digits elsewhere.

As mentioned earlier in the study that growing interest was the major cause of the financial crises the condition deteriorated and the banks which were functioning on zero interest bases were more stable.

With the study of literature on general studies it was found that Islamic banking has become the buzzword and it is in a nascent stage and there is an urgency to form an organisation that will assist in setting regulatory framework as well as an agenda in order to oversee Sharia financial institutions. Besides they further mentioned that training of Sharia banking and financial regulatory authorities and supervisors for better internal rating and controlling system for reducing risk which will result into improved external performance of the Sharia banks as well as would help them in capitalizing their equity funds more efficiently with increased growth and stability. Besides they explained few significant judicial issues that need to be solved to facilitate the better supervision of Sharia banking institutions and accelerate their growth rate. It also calls for facilities and assistance that are required to be provided to help these banks in order to overcome various issues and problems faced by them.

Some authors also suggested the viability of Islamic banks in India based on the success of Islamic banks in Muslim and Non Muslim countries. Literature suggested that Islamic Bank of Britain; Islamic banks of Thailand, Singapore and USA are brilliant examples to initiate Islamic banking practices in the India. It was advocated that the renowned national as well as international banks along with Reserve Bank of India must participate in the process of determination and execution of Islamic financial products in India. They referred "Islamic Banking" synonymous to "Interest Free Banking" so that it may be perceived rather through a broad economic perspective than a narrow religious vision.

Literature also suggests that there should be more awareness practices about Islamic banking as in countries where Islamic banking is functioning as the customers are not well versed with all the services and operations. Though customers prefer Islamic banking but there should be more awareness of the terms, functions, products, services, operations by the Islamic banks itself.

Also the literature indicates that there are certain doubts on the functioning of the Islamic banks as people see it as a complicated form of banking and think that there is a change in nomenclature and there could be presence of interest in this form of banking. Thus it is important that Islamic banks should make efforts in educating the people about its avoidance of interest from its products and services and also simplify the products and services for normal persons to understand. More initiatives to be taken in educating public for the fact of avoidance of interest and also for creating more and more opportunities for incorporating new techniques in the Islamic banks, so that they can survive with the traditional banking system.

The Western literature comprising economists like of Mills, Smith, Keynes, Minsky, Stiglitz, Friedman, Gertler who are the pioneers of Macro Economics also support interest free banking as the western economics is based on classical economics which has a basis of the perfect world but have made progress with the acceptance of uncertainty and imperfections and test economic theories empirically. It was also given that zero interest rate is a basic condition for optimal utilization of resources.

Based on the studies it was found that there is a need of Islamic banking in India as well and to know the prospects of Islamic study the present study is done. It is also important to know the banking system prevailing in India which is based on interest, the development of banking system, important acts through which the banks were functioning like the banking regulation Act, SIDBI Act, SBI Act, the major reforms like the Narsimham Committee. Then the functions performed by the banks with the change in technology the new additional services provided by the banks. The structure of the Banking System is also discussed with explanation of the role of RBI, Scheduled Commercial Banks, Non Scheduled Commercial Banks, Industrial Banks, Co-operative Banks, Foreign Banks, and Chit Funds and Indigenous banks. All these banks are functioning on the interest basis and for the purpose of introducing interest free banking there have to be made amendments in the present banking regulations or by inserting a clause in the present banking regulations.

In the fourth chapter the concept and practices of Islamic banking were highlighted. Also, the conditions of Islamic financial institutions which existed in India, their performances with the new regulations on NBFCs and the effect on the financial institutions. The decade of 1980s and 1990s saw proliferation of Islamic NBFCs. India's decision to introduce large-scale regulatory changes in the non-banking financial sector at a time when most of the South Asian countries were passing through severe economic recession did not promise well for the non-banking finance sector. More so Islamic NBFCs appears to have suffered more because of the distinct nature of their business and other religious constraints like not being able to avail the conventional avenues available to other financial institutions.

In a fast changing regulatory environment like this, a conventional NBFC would prefer keeping its money in commercial banks than to go with risk associated ventures that are part and parcel of Islamic financial institutions. On the other hand small size of Islamic NBFCs and a lack of the lender of last resort besides inexperienced and complacent attitude towards the regulation also had a fair share in their failures. Perhaps the recessionary economic phase could have easily been tackled, had the management been more alert and investors more informed.

Also the conditions of Islamic investments were discussed like the company should not be dealing in interest based borrowings more than 33%, receivables should not be more than 45% of the total assets. A list of such funds is also presented in chapter 3 of this study. The presence of Islamic banks worldwide also shows that Islamic banking is being adopted by most of the countries due to the benefits which can occur with the advent of Islamic banking like Inclusive Economic Growth, Growth of FDI, availability of funds for business, a system free from exploitation.

For availing such benefits there is a need to study the framework of the legal system in which it has to come into existence thus it is important to know the principles of Islamic banking, financial inclusion through Islamic banking as there is an issue of financial inclusion in India as per CRISIL also. The committees like Sachar Committee, Raghuram Rajan Committee have also mentioned about introducing Islamic banking in India for financial inclusion of Muslim community in India. But with the inception of Islamic banks in India there will be a number of challenges which will be in the way of Islamic banks like legal issues, risks associated. There are certain services which can be performed by the Islamic banks which will not violate the current regulations in the country. Islamic financial institutions have to be equally responsible to achieve financial stability through certain measures like corporate governance, management accountability, investors' protection and risk management. Islamic banking Framework in current banking regulation through Co-operative Societies as Al Khair Co-operative Society Ltd., Janseva Co-operative Credit Society Limited, Amanah Daily Fund Deposit, etc. Which have been working since the year 2010 till now is itself an achievement. The only thing which needs attention now is awareness of such products and services have to be brought as if people are not aware of such kinds of schemes, how will they support such initiatives? Thus more awareness drives have to be done in bringing awareness to the people of such organizations and also about the prohibition of interest in Islam and what disparities it can lead to should be informed to people.

7.2 Limitations of the Study

The limitations of the study are as follows:

1. The study is limited to a sample of 311 wherein 157 are Muslims and 154 are Non Muslims. Due to the limited time and the extent of scope of the study, an in depth study of each and every aspect of Islamic banking was not done.
2. The sample population of the present study has been taken from Delhi and NCR, which shows a different culture thus in case of generalization care needs to be taken.
3. The legal framework for banking industry in India is interest based, therefore the possibility of introducing zero interest banking require additional/amended laws.
4. In this study Muslims can be said as a part of a single culture. This can be said at the national level but there are cultural differences amongst different states of India. Thus more researches are needed for generalizing the findings to study the differences and its impact on the perception of Muslims in other regions of the country.

7.3 Suggestions

The following is the discussion on suggestions/recommendations made after conducting the present study:

1. As already discussed, most of the respondents are not aware of the terms of Islamic banking system, thus there is a need for an appropriate marketing model.
2. There are constraints in the implementation of Islamic banking in India due to the provisions in the Banking Regulations Act, special provisions could be created, on the lines of provisions for NBFCs, to permit Islamic banking in

India to attract resources from the Middle Eastern countries which will result in better infrastructure facilities and this in turn will drive the economic growth of the country. They also suggested that initially, experimentation with existing models could be carried out and then RBI can issue licenses to global players in a phased manner to drive growth. Islamic windows could be opened in such ventures by following the examples set by secular countries like US, UK, France and Germany and then finally full-fledged Islamic banks can be made operational.

3. It is important to create awareness that interest free banking is not only confined to a particular community, but is for all the people in the society. It is in fact an alternative banking model which has a profit and loss sharing model rendering interest free products and services.

4. There have been similar studies in Singapore and the UK which suggests that there could be a possibility of interest free services being provided with the opening of interest free windows in the commercial banks and by making certain amendments in the current regulatory framework in India.

5. There are also certain risks involved and care must be taken in mitigating the risks associated with Islamic banking while in the process of implementation. Some of the risks like financial risk, credit risk, interest rate risk, market risk, liquidity risk, settlement risk, etc should be taken care of during introduction and implementation of interest free banking in the country.

6. Investors' protection should be the primary concern and interest free banks should take such measures for ensuring the same like:

    a. High capital adequacy ratios should be there in Islamic financial institutions.

    b.   They should constitute depositors and shareholders protection funds.

    c.   They should constitute investment fluctuation reserves.

    d.   Contingency reserve should be created to face unforeseen events.

    e.   Risk management strategies have to be resorted to without compromising on the interest of depositors.

7. Management of risk is important in a business for its survival; more so in an Islamic bank as it is prescribed by the Sharia also. Not taking measures for the protection of wealth from certain risk is also one of the violations of Sharia. Thus it is recommended for an Islamic bank to set up a Risk management Committee for the management of credit and market risk.

The risk arising from over exposure to interconnected entities had been a threat for the existence of the financial institution in the past, thus the formation of a risk management committee should be strengthened in the institution.

The Risk committee should have arms length distance from executives involved in lending and investment. Financial Institutions, in the process are faced with various kinds of financial and non-financial risks like Credit risk, market risk (which includes foreign exchange risk, liquidity risk, equity price risk, commodity price risk legal risk, regulatory risk, reputational risk, operational risk etc). With the globalisation and liberalisation policies the entire financial system has become more integrated with the external markets, the risks thereof have become more complicated and require effective risk management. These risks are interrelated and thus can have an effect over a range of risk categories. Thus, Islamic institutions should have a careful assessment to measure, identify, monitor and control the overall risk.

In this context, Islamic financial institutions including banks are required to address all material kinds of risks in a planned way by advancement of their risk management skills and adopting more wide-ranging risk management practices.

8. Technological Challenges- It is very important in a scenario where ever changing technology is proving to be a great challenge for any business. To keep updated and to survive in the market it is important for the development of the required software and up gradation of services which are currently being provided by commercial banks in terms of ATMs, internet banking, mobile banking, etc.

So it is important that Islamic banking should prepare itself for a market wherein the customers are used to hassle free services by spending little time of theirs.

9. It is also vital that there should be a consensus in the scholars amongst Muslims regarding working of Islamic banking is concerned as there are certain critics of Islamic banking, and some are of the view that interest can be consumed if there are payments of taxes. So, a consensus should be reached in the light of Quran and Sunnah to take a decision in this regard and reach a consensus. The well known Sachar Committee in its report has also stated and suggested that Muslims in India belong to the marginalised group and do not have access to education, finance, and other amenities. It retreated that policies should "sharply focus on inclusive development and 'mainstreaming' of the Community while respecting diversity. It also suggested to determine the level of their socio-economic development and also to determine access to

education and health services, municipal infrastructure and bank credit provided by Government/ public sector entities.

The Sachar Committee has strong view for economic upliftment of Muslims by bringing them at the canvas of financial and banking environment. The development of the nation is not possible by giving power to a few people or class, for the development and progress of the nation it is important that all its inhabitants are having a good quality life and thus they can contribute in the growth of the economy.

10. The Financial Sector Reforms Committee (2007) which also mentioned about financial inclusion through interest free banking as can be seen from the excerpt of the report as- "Another area that falls broadly in the ambit of financial infrastructure for inclusion is the provision of interest-free banking. Certain faiths prohibit the use of financial instruments that pay interest. The non-availability of interest-free banking products (where the return to the investor is tied to the bearing of risk, in accordance with the principles of that faith) results in some Indians, including those in the economically disadvantaged strata of society, not being able to access banking products and services due to reasons of faith. This non-availability also denies India access to substantial sources of savings from other countries in the region.

While interest-free banking is provided in a limited manner through NBFCs and cooperatives, the Committee recommends that measures be taken to permit the delivery of interest-free finance on a larger scale, including through the banking system. This is in consonance with the objectives of inclusion and growth through innovation. The Committee believes that it would be possible, through appropriate measures, to create a framework for such products without any adverse systemic risk impact."

Thus, the prospects of Interest free banking i.e. Islamic Banking in India are bright. It can be launched for economic upliftment of all sections of the society specially the depressed sections of Muslim community.

7.4 Areas for Further Research

The following are the areas suggested for further research:

1. Holistic Approach- Islamic Finance has a lot of scope of research in future as in it's a new concept in India with regard to Indian economy as Islamic economics takes a comprehensive view of the human problems. This is an area where Islamic economics can make a contribution to the global pool of knowledge. (Khan, 1994) As Islamic finance will give the solution to human's life's issues thus it is important that one can take advice from Islamic economics to combat economic problems. Islamic Economics is a holistic approach of the human issues. Economists should not be content with raising such questions as: Is the firm profitable? Is there full employment? Are prices stable? Is the growth rate satisfactory? Instead, they should also ask questions regarding human, psychological, motivational and environmental needs. They should also see in which way the economy is deviating from the path of human success. Thus more studies can be done keeping in mind the holistic approach of Islamic banking. For example the relevant questions regarding introduction of technology: How does it affect the employment of those already in the job? How will it prevent those who are seeking jobs so as to enter the labor market? Who will pay for the retraining and rehabilitation of those misplaced? How will the new technology affect the quality of life of

those who will work under the new conditions? What type of stress and strain will it bring? What effect will it have on international market? Also the traditional economics has treated most of such questions as exogenous. While these questions if considered will give a comprehensive view of the human problems. This is an area where Islamic Economics can make a contribution to the global pool of knowledge.

2. Search for an Interest free International Economic Order- The benefits of the interest free system working on a basis of an environment which is entirely free of interest can be experienced. So the countries which are completely interest free can be studied for the purpose of knowing the payback of an interest free system. The challenge before the economists of the world is to find out an institutional mechanism which provides finance free of interest so that the idle resources of the world are used for the benefit of humanity. The day humanity is able to abolish interest effectively will be the day of its real liberation. The abolition of interest would mean what Keynes has rightly termed as a 'sea change'.

3. More studies can be done in other parts of the country to reach a consensus of the prospects of Islamic banking.

4. The models of countries like the UK, Singapore, Malaysia, etc. can be studied and similar models can be used for Islamic banking in India as these countries also had a lateral entry in the banking structure.

5. The amendments in regulations made for Islamic banking in the countries where it had no presence can also be studied.

Appendix 1

Questionnaire on Islamic Banking in India

Awareness

Read the following statement in the sections regarding awareness about Islamic methods of finance. Mark your degree of agreement from 1 to 5 where "1" is "Strongly disagree" and "5" is "Strongly agree".

AW1*RequiredI am aware of the existence of Islamic Banks that apply Islamic methods of finance worldwide.

              1   2   3   4   5

Strongly Disagree ☐ ☐ ☐ ☐ ☐ Strongly Agree

AW2*RequiredIslamic Banks are based on Sharia (Islamic law)

              1   2   3   4   5

Strongly Disagree ☐ ☐ ☐ ☐ ☐ Strongly Agree

AW3*RequiredRiba is prohibited in Islam, thus Islamic Banks do not deal in Riba.

              1   2   3   4   5

Strongly Disagree ☐ ☐ ☐ ☐ ☐ Strongly Agree

AW4*RequiredI have knowledge of Islamic methods of finance that is loan on the basis of only profit sharing by the client having expertise and loss is borne by the bank, which invests capital (Mudarabah).

1　2　3　4　5

Strongly Disagree ☐ ☐ ☐ ☐ ☐ Strongly Agree

AW5*Required I have knowledge of Islamic methods of finance that is loan on the basis of profit and loss sharing (Musharakah)

1　2　3　4　5

Strongly Disagree ☐ ☐ ☐ ☐ ☐ Strongly Agree

AW6*Required I have knowledge of Islamic methods of finance (Murabahah) which is an acceptable form of credit sale under Sharia.

1　2　3　4　5

Strongly Disagree ☐ ☐ ☐ ☐ ☐ Strongly Agree

AW7*Required I have knowledge of Islamic methods of finance (Bai Muajjal) installment sale of goods arranged by bank.

1　2　3　4　5

Strongly Disagree ☐ ☐ ☐ ☐ ☐ Strongly Agree

AW8*Required I have knowledge of Islamic methods of finance (Bai Salam) a contract in which advance payment is made for goods to be delivered at a future date, following Islam and Islamic shariah.

1　2　3　4　5

Strongly Disagree ☐ ☐ ☐ ☐ ☐ Strongly Agree

AW9*RequiredI have knowledge of Islamic methods of finance (Istisna) financing of manufacturing of goods and equipment, as well as in the financing of construction works.

                        1   2   3   4   5

Strongly Disagree ☐ ☐ ☐ ☐ ☐ Strongly Agree

AW10*RequiredI have knowledge of Islamic methods of finance (Ijarah) Lease.

                        1   2   3   4   5

Strongly Disagree ☐ ☐ ☐ ☐ ☐ Strongly Agree

AW11*RequiredI have knowledge of Islamic methods of finance(Qard Hasana)Benevolent Loans.

                        1   2   3   4   5

Strongly Disagree ☐ ☐ ☐ ☐ ☐ Strongly Agree

AW12*RequiredI do not have knowledge of any Islamic methods of finance.

                        1   2   3   4   5

Strongly Disagree ☐ ☐ ☐ ☐ ☐ Strongly Agree

Motivating Factors

If Islamic Banks open up in India to apply Islamic methods of finance, which of the following reasons might motivate you to use their Islamic methods of finance? Mark the importance from 1 to 5 where "1" is " Not Important at all" and "5" is " extremely important"

MF1*RequiredInterest free methods of finance.

                     1   2   3   4   5

Not important at all ☐ ☐ ☐ ☐ ☐   Extremely important

MF2*RequiredIslamic methods of finance in accordance with Islamic Sharia

                     1   2   3   4   5

Not important at all ☐ ☐ ☐ ☐ ☐   Extremely important

MF3*RequiredRealisation of higher and variable rate of return on deposits

                     1   2   3   4   5

Not important at all ☐ ☐ ☐ ☐ ☐   Extremely important

MF4*RequiredReligious motivation for depositing/ borrowing with Islamic bank

                     1   2   3   4   5

Not important at all ☐ ☐ ☐ ☐ ☐   Extremely important

MF5*RequiredCost of borrowing not being fixed but depending on the outcome of the business

                     1   2   3   4   5

Not important at all ☐ ☐ ☐ ☐ ☐   Extremely important

MF6*RequiredInvesting with according to profit sharing method only (Mudarabah)

              1   2   3   4   5

Not important at all ☐ ☐ ☐ ☐ ☐ Extremely important

MF7*Required Repayment of debt in accordance with the current financial condition of the business

              1   2   3   4   5

Not important at all ☐ ☐ ☐ ☐ ☐ Extremely important

MF8*Required Lending of money according to profit/ loss sharing (Musharakah)

              1   2   3   4   5

Not important at all ☐ ☐ ☐ ☐ ☐ Extremely important

MF9*Required Sharing of business risk

              1   2   3   4   5

Not important at all ☐ ☐ ☐ ☐ ☐ Extremely important

MF10*Required Business management support from the Islamic bank

              1   2   3   4   5

Not important at all ☐ ☐ ☐ ☐ ☐ Extremely important

MF11*Required Encourages business innovation as well as expansion

              1   2   3   4   5

Not important at all ☐ ☐ ☐ ☐ ☐ Extremely important

MF12*RequiredImproves business efficiency

                1   2   3   4   5

Not important at all ☐ ☐ ☐ ☐ ☐ Extremely important

MF13*RequiredProvide lease financing(Ijarah)

                1   2   3   4   5

Not important at all ☐ ☐ ☐ ☐ ☐ Extremely important

MF14*RequiredTrade and Industrial financing(Murabaha and Istisna)

                1   2   3   4   5

Not important at all ☐ ☐ ☐ ☐ ☐ Extremely important

Attitude

Read the following statements in sections regarding attitudes, application and implementation of Islamic methods of finance. Mark your degree of agreement from 1 to 5 where "1" is "strongly disagree" and "5" is "strongly agree".

AT1*RequiredScope for interest free bank is limited in state as people are already using commercial banks and are satisfied with the system.

                1   2   3   4   5

Strongly disagree ☐ ☐ ☐ ☐ ☐ Strongly agree

AT2*RequiredOnly educated people having knowledge of Islamic principles may switch the accounts from interest free banks to conventional banks

1 2 3 4 5

Strongly disagree ☐ ☐ ☐ ☐ ☐ Strongly agree

AT3*RequiredInterest free bank will provide the return to you which will be acceptable to you

1 2 3 4 5

Strongly disagree ☐ ☐ ☐ ☐ ☐ Strongly agree

AT4*RequiredOnly people having insufficient knowledge of Islamic principles but having complete faith in Islam will switch their accounts from commercial banks to interest free banks

1 2 3 4 5

Strongly disagree ☐ ☐ ☐ ☐ ☐ Strongly agree

AT5*RequiredThe performance of Interest free bank will be better even during the financial meltdown

1 2 3 4 5

Strongly disagree ☐ ☐ ☐ ☐ ☐ Strongly agree

AT6*RequiredInterest free banks will provide diversified banking services based on customer needs

1 2 3 4 5

Strongly disagree ☐ ☐ ☐ ☐ ☐ Strongly agree

AT7*Required An interest free bank, if started in India will drive majority of population banking with them.

1 2 3 4 5

Strongly disagree ☐ ☐ ☐ ☐ ☐ Strongly agree

Application

Islamic methods of finance can also be practiced between individuals, which of them have you practised yourself?

AP1*Required I have been practising the Islamic methods of finance myself (Mudarabah) only profit sharing

1 2 3 4 5

Strongly Disagree ☐ ☐ ☐ ☐ ☐ Strongly Agree

AP2*Required I have been practising the Islamic methods of finance myself (Musharakah) profit/loss sharing.

1 2 3 4 5

Strongly Disagree ☐ ☐ ☐ ☐ ☐ Strongly Agree

AP3*Required I have been practising the Islamic methods of finance myself (Murabahah) which is an acceptable form of credit sale under Sharia.

1 2 3 4 5

Strongly Disagree ☐ ☐ ☐ ☐ ☐ Strongly Agree

AP4*RequiredI have been practising the Islamic methods of finance myself (Bai Muajjal) installment sale of goods arranged by bank.

1　2　3　4　5

Strongly Disagree ☐ ☐ ☐ ☐ ☐ Strongly Agree

AP5*RequiredI have been practising the Islamic methods of finance myself (Bai Salam) a contract in which advance payment is made for goods to be delivered at a future date, following Islam and Islamic shariah.

1　2　3　4　5

Strongly Disagree ☐ ☐ ☐ ☐ ☐ Strongly Agree

AP6*RequiredI have been practising the Islamic methods of finance myself (Istisna) financing of manufacturing of goods and equipment, as well as in the financing of construction works.

1　2　3　4　5

Strongly Disagree ☐ ☐ ☐ ☐ ☐ Strongly Agree

AP7*RequiredI have been practising the Islamic methods of finance myself (Ijara) lease financing.

1　2　3　4　5

Strongly Disagree ☐ ☐ ☐ ☐ ☐ Strongly Agree

AP8*RequiredI Have been practising the Islamic methods of finance myself (Qard Hasan) benevolent loans.

                1   2   3   4   5

Strongly Disagree ☐ ☐ ☐ ☐ ☐ Strongly Agree

AP9*Required i have not been practising any Islamic methods of finance myself.

                1   2   3   4   5

Strongly Disagree ☐ ☐ ☐ ☐ ☐ Strongly Agree

AP10*Required I have been utilizing the interest from commercial banks or investments for personal use

                1   2   3   4   5

Strongly Disagree ☐ ☐ ☐ ☐ ☐ Strongly Agree

AP11*Required i have been taking out the interest from commercial banks or investments and giving it in charity.

                1   2   3   4   5

Strongly Disagree ☐ ☐ ☐ ☐ ☐ Strongly Agree

AP12*Required I ensure that the schemes I choose for investment should be interest free.

                1   2   3   4   5

Strongly Disagree ☐ ☐ ☐ ☐ ☐ Strongly Agree

Implementation

IM1*Required If Islamic banks open up in India, I would like to use their Islamic methods of finance

1 2 3 4 5

Strongly Disagree ☐ ☐ ☐ ☐ ☐ Strongly Agree

IM2*Required Do you agree that if more branches of Islamic banking institutions open up throughout a country, more people will utilize the services provided by these banks.

1 2 3 4 5

Strongly Disagree ☐ ☐ ☐ ☐ ☐ Strongly Agree

IM3*Required In case an Islamic bank announced that it had no profit to distribute on investment and savings deposits for any one year, if I were a depositor, I would keep the deposit at the same or a different Islamic bank, because placing the deposit with a non-Islamic bank contravenes Islamic principles

1 2 3 4 5

Strongly Disagree ☐ ☐ ☐ ☐ ☐ Strongly Agree

IM4*Required Do you agree that the granting of interest-free loans by Islamic banks is considered a contribution on the part of the bank to help the community in a just and efficient manner.

1 2 3 4 5

Strongly Disagree ☐ ☐ ☐ ☐ ☐ Strongly Agree

IM5*Required Interest Free banking is going to be safer as it would be regulated by the government as well as Sharia (Islamic Law).

1 2 3 4 5

Strongly Disagree ☐ ☐ ☐ ☐ ☐ Strongly Agree

IM6*Required If interest free banking facilities are being provided in India it will create more investment opportunities for interest averse people from abroad and within the country.

1 2 3 4 5

Strongly Disagree ☐ ☐ ☐ ☐ ☐ Strongly Agree

IM7*Required Interest free bank will help in generating more employment opportunities and wealth amongst people.

1 2 3 4 5

Strongly Disagree ☐ ☐ ☐ ☐ ☐ Strongly Agree

Demographic Factors

Please check as applicable

Gender*Required

- ☐ Male
- ☐ Female

Age*Required

- ☐ <25

- ☐ 26-35
- ☐ 36-45
- ☐ 46-55
- ☐ 56 or above

Education*Required

- ☐ Undergraduate
- ☐ Graduate
- ☐ Post Graduate
- ☐ Doctorate and above

Occupation*Required

- ☐ Private
- ☐ Public
- ☐ Self Employed
- ☐ Retired
- ☐ Other:

Religion*Required

- ☐ Muslim
  - ☐ Non Muslim

BIBLIOGRAPHY

Books:

1. Ahmad, K. (1998). Islam and Challenge of Economic Development. Redwood Burn Ltd.: London. pp.111-113
2. Gafoor, A. (1995). *Interest-free Commercial Banking.* Apptec Publications: Netherlands. pp. 347-352
3. Haron, S., and Shanmugan, B. (1997). *Islamic Banking System, Concepts and Applications.* Palanduk Publications: Malaysia. pp. 168-171
4. Homoud, S. (1985). *Islamic Banking.* Arabian Information Ltd.: London. pp. 547
5. Iqbal, Z., and Mirakhor, A. (1987). *Islamic Banking.* International Monetary Fund : Washington, D.C. pp.121-124
6. Khan, Mohsen. (1998).*Principles of Monetary theory and Policy in an Islamic Framework.* International Institute of Islamic Economics: Pakistan. pp.67-70
7. Mirakhor, A., & Iqbal, Zaidi. (1988). Stabilization and Growth in an Open Islamic Economy. International Monetary Fund: Washington, D.C.pp.76-79
8. Mirakhor, A. (1999). *The Progress of Islamic Banking.* University of London: London. pp.128-130
9. Musavian, S.A. (2004). *Islamic Banking.* Monetary and Research Academy of Central Bank of the Islamic Republic of Iran: Iran. p. 144
10. Muslehuddin, M. (2003). Insurance and Islamic Law. Islamic publications Ltd.: Lahore. pp.99-102
11. Siddiqui, M.N. (1981). *Banking without Interest.* Islamic Publications: Lahore. p.421
12. Schacht, J. (1995). *Reba in The Encyclopedia of Islam.* Leiden: Netherlands. pp.397
13. Schacht, J. (1994). *An Introduction to Islamic Law.* Clarendon Pres: Oxford. pp. 146-147
14. Wilson, R. (1990). *Islamic Financial Markets.* Routledge: London.

Reports
1. Annual Report of Islamic Development Bank, 2014.
2. Report of the Committee on Financial Sector Reforms, Sage Publications, 2009, New Delhi.
3. Summary of Sachar Committee Report.

Doctoral Theses
1. Kumar, Praveen, 2015, Financial Performance of Scheduled Commercial Banks in India: An Analysis, India.
2. Mir, Shabir Mushtaq, 2015, A study of perception and attitudes of Stakeholders towards Islamic banking in India, University of Kashmir, India.
3. Prajapati, Sangita R,2013, An Indepth study of profitability and prospects of selected private sector banks in India, India.

Conference Proceedings
1. Faisal, M., Akhtar, A., & Rehman, A. (2012, December 17,18). Awareness of Islamic Banking in India –An empirical study. Retrieved April 14, 2013, from www.wbiconpro.com: http://www.wbiconpro.com/606-Faisal.pdf
2. Nisar, S (2004), Islamic Non Banking Financial Institutions in India: Special Focus on Regulation, Seminar on Non bank Financial Institutions: Islamic Alternatives, 1-3 March, 2004, Kuala Lumpur.

Journals and Periodicals

1. Abalkhail, M. and Presley, J.R. (2002), How informal risk capital investors manage asymmetric information in profit/loss-sharing contracts, in Iqbal, M. and Llewellyn, D.T. (2002), Islamic Banking and Finance, New Perspectives on Profit-Sharing and Risk. Edward Elgar, Cheltenham, UK, Northampton, MA, USA, 111-134.
2. Abdallah, A. (1987). Islamic Banking. *Journal of Islamic Banking and Finance*, *04*(01), pp. 31-56
3. Abdullah, A., Sidek, R., & Adnan, A. (2012). Perception of non-Muslim Customers towards Islamic banks in Malaysia. *International Journal of Business and Social Science*, 151-163.
4. Ahmad. Z. (1987). Interest free Banking in Iran. *Journal of Islamic Banking and Finance*, *04*(02), pp. 8-30.

5. Ahamed, W., Rahman, A., Ali, N., & Seman, A. (2008). Religiosity and banking selection criteria amongst Malays in Malaysia. *Journal Syria,* 279-304.
6. Ahangar, G., Padder, M., & Ganie, A. (2013). Islamic Banking and its scope in India. *International Journal of Commerce, Business and Management,* 266-269.
7. Ahmad, K. (2012). Feasibility of Islamic banking as an alternative to conventional banking in India. *Online International Interdisciplinary Research Journal, 02* (02). Retrieved from http://www.oiirj.org/oiirj/mar2012/07.pdf
8. Alam, M. (2000). Islamic banking in Bangladesh: A case study of IBBL. *International Journal of Islamic financial services,* 10-29.
9. Amin, A. (2012). Islamic banking in India: Religious and socio-economic perspective affecting Muslim investors of Ahmedabad district in Gujarat. *International Journal of research in Commerce, IT and Management,* 116-121.
10. Asif, M., & Anjum, M. (2012). Acceptance of Islamic banking in Muslim Customers. *International Review of Management and Business Research,* 9-17.
11. Awan, H., & Bukhari, K. (2011). Customer's criteria for selecting an Islamic bank: Evidence From Pakistan. *Journal of Islamic Marketing,* 14-27.
12. Badruddin, A. (2015). Islamic Banking and Finance in India - Kosher or Myth. *International Journal of Management, Innovation and Entrepreneurial Research,* 1-9
13. Bagsiraj, M. (2003). *Islamic Financial Institutions of India: Progress, Problems and Prospects.* Riyadh: King Abdul Azeez University.
14. Basha N.S., & Ahmed, B.(2013), Relevance of Islamic Banking to Indian Economy. *International Journal of Research in Commerce, IT and Management,* 17-20.
15. Bhat, Z. (2013). Nature, Scope and Feasibility of Islamic Banking in India. *Abhinav Journal,* 121-126.
16. Bley, J., & Kuehn, K. (2004). Conventional versus Islamic Finance: student knowledge and Perception in the United Arab Emirates. *International Journal of Islamic Financial Services,* 17-30.

17. Chebab, S., & Zribi, H. (2012). Expected Regret and Islamic banking in emerging countries: The case of Tunisia. *Journal of Business Studies Quarterly*, 119-131.
18. Dusuki, A., & Abdullah, N. (2007). Why do Malaysian Customers patronize Islamic banks? *International Journal of Bank Marketing*, 142-160.
19. Erol, C., & El-Bdour, R. (1989). Attitudes, Behaviour and patronage factors of bank Customers towards Islamic banks. *International Journal of Bank Marketing*, 6.
20. Erol, C., Kaynak, E., & El Bdour, R. (1990). Conventional and Islamic Banks: patronage behaviour of Jordanian customers. *International Journal of Bank Marketing*, 4.
21. Fada, K., & Wabekwa, B. (2012). Peoples' Perception towards Islamic banking : A fieldwork study in Gombe LGA, Nigeria. *International Journal of Business, Humanities and Technology*, 121-131.
22. Gerrard, P., & Cunningham, B. (1997). Islamic banking: A study in Singapore. *International Journal of Bank Marketing*, 153-216.
23. Greenwald, B. C. and Stiglitz, J. E. (1988). "Money, Imperfect Information and Economic Fluctuations" in Dar, A. H. and Presley, J. R. (1999). "Islamic Finance: A Western Perspective", International Journal of Islamic Financial Services, Vol. 1 No. 1.
24. Guyo, W., & Adan, N. (2013). The determinants of Retail consumer choice of Islamic banking in Kenya. *International journal of Arts and Entrepreneurship*, 1-12.
25. Haque, A. (2010). Islamic Banking in Malaysia: A study on Attitudinal difference of Malaysian Customers. *European Journal of Economics, Finance and Administrative services*, 7-18.
26. Haque, A., Osman, J., & Ismail, A. (2009). Factors Influencing selection of Islamic banking: *A study on Malaysian Customer Preferences. American Journal of Applied Sciences*, 922-928.
27. Haron, S., Ahmad, N., & Planisek, S. (1994). Bank Patronage factors of Muslim and non Muslim customers. *International Journal of Bank Marketing*, 32-40.

28. Hidayat, S., & Al Bawardi, N. (2013). Non-Muslims' perceptions towards Islamic banking service in Saudi Arabia. *Journal of US-China Public Administration*, 654-670.
29. Hin, C., Wei, C., Bohari, A., & Adam, M. (2011). Bank Selection criteria and service Quality of Islamic banking: A comparison between Muslim and non-Muslim students and its effects on students' satisfaction. *Jurnal Eknonom*, 104-114.
30. Idris, A., Naziman, K., Januri, S., Asari, F., Muhammad, N., Sabri, S., et al. (2011). Religious value as main influencing factor to customers patronizing Islamic bank. *World Applied Sciences Journal*, 8-13.
31. Jammeh, B. E. (2010). Prospects and Challenges of Islamic Banking in USA. *Journal of Social Science Research Network*.
32. Jamshidi, D., Hussin, N., & Wan, H. (2013). The potential impact of demographic items On Islamic banking services : Acceptance and usage- A literature review. *International Journal of Social Science and Humanities Research*, 34-39.
33. Kader, R., Zakaria, R., Razali, N., & Abdullah, N. (2014). Why this Bank? Understanding Customers' preference for an Islamic bank in a competitive market. *Journal of Islamic Economics, Banking and Finance*, 138-153.
34. Khader, A. & Idris, M. (2016). A feasibility study on Islamic banking in India. *IRACST – International Journal of Commerce, Business and Management (IJCBM)*. Retrieved from http://www.iracst.org/ijcbm/papers/vol5no52016/2vol5no5.pdf
35. Khalidi, M. A., and Amanaullah (2010), Consumer perception of Islamic banking in Pakistan. *Labuan bulletin of international business & finance*, 1-21.
36. Khan, K.A., (2013), Emerging Islamic Banking: Its need and scope in India. *Pacific Business Review International*, 84-90.
37. Khattak, N., & Rehman, K. (2010). Customer Satisfaction and awareness of Islamic Banking system in Pakistan. *African Journal of Business Management*, 662-670.
38. Khoirunissa, D. (2003). Consumers' preference towards Islamic banking. *Journal of Islamic Economics*, 145-168.

39. Loo, M. (2010). Attitudes and Perception towards Islamic banking among Muslims and Non Muslims in Malaysia. *International Journal of Arts and Sciences,* 453-485.
40. Malik, A., Malik, M. S., & Shah, H. (2011). Analysis of Islamic banking and finance in West: From Lagging to Leading. *Asian Social Science,* 179-185.
41. Marimuthu, M., Jing, C., Gie, L., Mun, L., & Ping, T. (2010). Islamic banking: Selection criteria and Implications. *Global Journal of Human Social Science,* 52-62.
42. Matthews, R. Tlemsani and Siddique A (2004) Islamic banking and the mortgage market in the UK, in Shanmugam, Balaet.al (Eds) (2004). Islamic banking: an international perspective, Serdang, Malaysia: university Putra Malaysia press.
43. Metawa, S., & Al Mossawi, M. (1998). Banking Behaviour of Islamic Bank customers: Perspectives and implications. *International Journal of Bank Marketing,* 299-313.
44. Metwally, M. (2002). The impact of demographic factors on consumer's selection of a particular bank within a dual banking system: A case study. *Journal of International Marketing and Marketing Research,* 35-44.
45. Minsky, H. P. (1977). A Theory of Systematic Fragility, in Dar, A. H. and Presley, J. R. (1999), Islamic Finance: A Western Perspective. *International Journal of Islamic Financial Services.*
46. Mirakhor, A. (1989). Islamic Banking: Experiences in the Islamic Republic of Iran and Pakistan. *International Monetary Fund (IMF),* January 30, IMF Working Paper No. 89/12, p.21
47. Mirakhor, A. (1987). Analysis of Short-Term Asset Concentration in Islamic Banking. *International Monetary Fund (IMF),* October 8, IMF Working Paper No. 87/67, pp. 14
48. Muniswamy, S., Soundararajan, G., & Ramasamy, R. (2013). Islamic Finance in India: A study on the perception of College Teachers in India. *Journal of Islamic Economics, Banking and Finance,* 131-148.
49. Naser, K., Jamal, A., & Al-Khatib, K. (1999). Islamic banking: A study of customer satisfaction and preference in Jordan. *International journal of bank marketing,* 135-150.

50. Okumus, H. (2005). Interest-free banking in Turkey: a study of customer satisfaction and Bank selection criteria. *Journal of Economic co-operation*, 51-86.
51. Okumus, H., & Genc, E. (2013). Interest free banking in Turkey: A study on customer Satisfaction and Bank selection. *European Scientific Journal*, 144-166.
52. Pandu, A., & Hussain, M. G. (2011). Introduction of Islamic banking in India: A Suggested legal framework. *International Journal of Research in commerce, economics and management*, 117-120.
53. Rahman, S. M., Islam, M. S., & Akter, T. (2013). Demographic Profile of the customers and their level of satisfaction: a study of IBBL. *Research journal of finance and accounting*, 28-38.
54. Ramadan, Z. (2013). Jordanian criteria for Islamic Bank selection- Evidence from the Jordanian Banking Sector. *International Journal of Academic research in Accounting, Finance and Management sciences*, 139-145.
55. Ramdhony, D. (2013). Islamic banking- Awareness, attitude and bank selection criteria. *International Journal of Humanities and Applied Sciences*, 29-35.
56. Rammal, H., & Zurbruegg, R. (2007). Awareness of Islamic banking products among Muslims: The case of Australia. *Journal of Financial Services Marketing*, 65-74.
57. Rao, A., & Sharma, R. (2010). Bank Selection criteria employed by MBA Students in Delhi: An empirical Analysis. *Journal of Business studies Quarterly*, 56-69.
58. Rasheed, H., Aimin, W., & Ahmed, A. (2012). An Evaluation of Bank Customer Satisfaction in Pakistan, Comparing foreign and Islamic banks. *International Journal of Academic Research in Business and Social science*, 177-184.
59. Rashid, M., & Hassan, K. (2009). Customer Demographics affecting Bank selection criteria, preferences and market segmentation: Study on Domestic Islamic banks in Bangladesh. *International Journal of Business and Management*.
60. Redimerio, & Andrew. (2011). Will Islamic finance play a key role in funding Asia's Huge Infrastructure task? Standard and Poors.

61. Rustam, S., Bibi, S., Zaman, K., Rustam, A., & Huq, Z. (2011). Perception of Corporate customers towards Islamic banking products and services in Pakistan. *The Romanian Economic Journal*, 107-123.
62. Saad, N. (2012). Comparative Analysis of Customer satisfaction on Islamic and Conventional banks in Malaysia. *Asian Social science*, 73-77.
63. Selamat, Z., & Kadir, H. A. (2012). Attitude and patronage factors of bank customers in Malaysia: Muslim and non-Muslim views. *Journal of Islamic Economics, banking and finance*, 87-99.
64. Sheik, R., & Ahammad, M. (2013). The feasibility of establishing Islamic banks in the UK: the case of Nottingham. *International Journal of Social Entrepreneurship and Innovation*, 67-82.
65. Singh, V. G., & Kaur, N. (2014). Islamic Banking- In Indian Context. *International journal of Emerging research in management & Technology*, 25-31.
66. Singh, J., & Yadav, P. (2013). Islamic Banking in India - Growth and Potential. *International Journal of Marketing, Financial Services and Management Research*, 59-77.
67. Subhani, M., Hasan, S., Rafiq, M., Nayaz, M., & Osman, A. (2012). Consumer criteria for the selection of Islamic banks: Evidence from Pakistan. *International Research Journal of Finance and Economics*.
68. Thambiah, S., Eze, U., Shantapparaj, A. J., & Arumugam, K. (2011). Customers' perception of Islamic retail banking: A comparative analysis between the urban and rural regions of Malaysia. *International Journal of Business and Management*, 187-197.
69. Tripathy, M., (2009) Inclusive Banking. Frontline Oct 23, 2009
70. Vasu, B., (2005). 'Islamic Banking- Banking for a change'. The Indian Express, October 2, 2005.
71. Yatoo, N., & Sudalaimuthu, S. (2013). What the Indian Muslims think about Islamic Finance: A empirical study. *International Journal of Research in Computer Application and Management*, 68-69.
72. Yatoo, N. A. (2013). Islamic finance in India: An assessment of idea and awareness. *International journal of Islamic banking and finance*, 1-10

73. Yusuf, M., & Shamsuddin, A. (n.d.). Muslim Consumers' attitude towards Islamic Finance Products in a non-Muslim country. *Jurnal Kemanusiaan*, 94-103.

Websites

1. Analysis of Short- Term Asset Concentration in Islamic Banking. Retrieved from www.Islamic_finance.net
2. bank. (n.d.) Farlex Financial Dictionary. (2009). Retrieved December 13 2016 from http://financial-dictionary.thefreedictionary.com/bank.
3. CRISIL http://crisil.com/pdf/corporate/CRISIL-Inclusix.pdf, CRISIL,2013
4. Humble, 2015 Muslim Mirror. http://muslimmirror.com/eng/janseva-co-operative-credit-society-a-step-in-the-islamic-finance-and-banking-in-india/ 17/12/2016.
5. Indian Microcredit faces collapse from defaults: Retrieved from http://www.nytimes.com/2010/11/18/world/asia/18micro.html?pagewanted=all&_r=0 New York Times, 2010.
6. Islamic Microfinance Scale, CGAPhttp://www.cgap.org/blog/taking-islamic-microfinance-scale
7. Islamic Banking: Experiences in the Islamic Republic of Iran and Pakistan. Retrieved from www.emeraldinsight.com
8. Islamic Banking: Interest- Free or Interest- Based? Retrieved from www.amerricanfinance.com
9. Islamic Banking; Issues in Prudential Regulations and Supervision. Retrieved from www.papers.ssrn.com
10. Islamic banks can better serve the poor: https://www.devex.com/news/abdul-halim-bin-ismail-how-islamic-banks-can-better-serve-the-poor-86061. Retrieved in December, 2015.
11. Islamic banking keeps Iran recession-proof.www.thebanker.com, 04, August 2009 Issue.
12. Islamic Financial Institutions Products in the Global Financial System: Key Issues in Risk Management and Challenges Ahead. Retrieved from www.springerlink.com
13. Khan M Y (2010) Islamic banks and regulatory framework in india, 2010, Islamitijara.com,

http://pragmaticwealth.net/KnowledgeCentre/PDF/Islamic%20Banks%20and%20Regulatory%20Framework%20in%20India.pdf 17-12-2016.

14. Kustin Bridget,2015 http://www.impatientoptimists.org/Posts/2015/10/The-promise-of-Islamic-finance--user-experiences-product-innovation-and-the-potential-for-poverty-alleviation

15. Monetary Operations and Government Debt Management under Islamic Banking. Retrieved from www.luk.edu.org

16. Social Reporting by Islamic Banks. Retrieved from www.ideas.repec.org

17. Value through Diversity: Microfinance and Islamic Finance and Global Banking. Retrieved from www.financeinislam.com

www.ingramcontent.com/pod-product-compliance
Lightning Source LLC
LaVergne TN
LVHW010202070526
838199LV00062B/4459